Namibia
in the 1980s

Namibia in the 1980s

The Catholic Institute for International Relations
and
The British Council of Churches

First published in October 1981 by
Catholic Institute for International Relations, 1 Cambridge Terrace,
London NW1, and
British Council of Churches, 2 Eaton Gate, London SW1

ISBN 0 904393 58 5

Namibia in the 1980s
 1. Namibia — Politics and government
 2. Namibia — History
 I. Catholic Institute for International Relations
 II. British Council of Churches
 968.8′ 03 DT714
 ISBN 0 904393 58 5

Copies available by post from CIIR and BCC. Trade distribution to
bookshops and library supplies by Third World Publications Ltd,
151 Stratford Road, Birmingham B11 1RD, Tel. 021-773 6572.

Printed by the Russell Press Ltd, Bertrand Russell House, Nottingham
(UK).
Design by Jan Brown 01-485 9009.

Contents

Map of Namibia

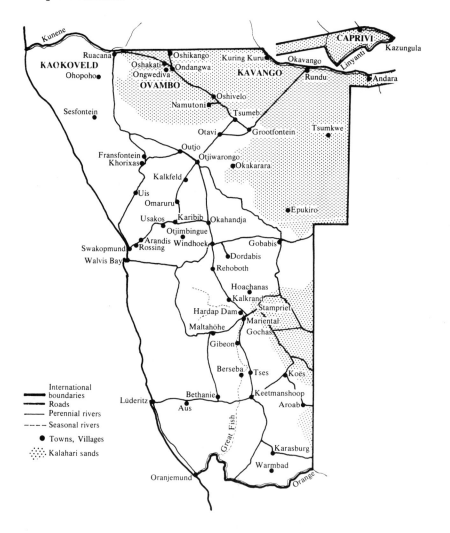

Foreword

It is now over a decade since the ruling of the International Court of Justice that the South African occupation of Namibia is illegal. The conclusion of this 1971 ruling, that South Africa should withdraw from Namibia, is no less valid today. Ten years of fruitless negotiations have not altered the simple basis for a solution to the 'Namibia problem'; the only legal action open to South Africa is to leave the territory.

The 'Namibia problem' is a South Africa problem. Not only has South Africa openly defied the consensus of the international community in augmenting the number of her troops in Namibia to massive proportions, but she has pursued a 'national solution', bringing into existence an illegal regime incapable of governing effectively, the DTA. The illegality of the South African occupation has thus been compounded and complicated while a major war now escalates both in northern Namibia and in southern Angola.

The problem of the South African occupation of Namibia is essentially one of international law and international order, rightly in the hands of the United Nations. But it is much more. Namibia shows in exaggerated form the deformities of a colonial economy, the ravages of the apartheid system given free rein for two decades, and the product of state violence, a population in revolt supporting a war of liberation whose interests are often the last to be considered.

These are matters of grave concern for the world community and for the Christian churches. As a mandated territory illegally 'annexed' by South Africa since the late 1940s, Namibia is a responsibility that should lie heavily on the conscience of the international community. This conscience has been expressed in repeated resolutions of the United Nations Security Council and General Assembly, by the World Council of Churches and by the Christian churches in Namibia and their sister churches around the world. But no immediate end to the suffering of the Namibian people is in sight. Major western powers, amongst others, persist in illegal purchases of Namibia's mineral resources while reluctance to adopt sanctions weakens diplomatic pressure.

The blocking of Namibian independence by South Africa has now created a complex situation threatening the peace of the south-western region of the continent. There is an ever more pressing need for a rapid implementation of the UN proposals to move into free and fair elections under UN supervision, set out in Resolution 435 passed by the Security Council in 1978. Yet growing evidence suggests that powerful military voices in South Africa now seek outright military victory in Namibia rather than a 'political solution'.

The purpose of this publication is therefore twofold: to draw the attention of Christian opinion outside Namibia to the gravity of the expanding war in northern Namibia and southern Angola and to highlight the responsibility of the west, in particular the Contact Group of five western nations, to return the territory to legality; secondly to provide a concise account of how the contemporary conflict arose, the situation in Namibia today, and where hopes for the future lie.

To provide this account it is necessary first to sketch in the tortured and tortuous history of Namibia in the 1970s, before going on to an analysis of Namibia in the 1980s. Readers well acquainted with Namibia may therefore move rapidly to Chapter 2.

CIIR and the BCC have been privileged to have contribute to this publication a wide range of experts in the history and political economy of Namibia, several of whom have been actively involved in the events described in the text. But equally important have been discussions taking place over an extended period of time with Christians and non-Christians, both in Namibia and in exile. It is above all the insights of both black and white Namibians, particularly from the Christian community, which has increasingly played a leading role in the nationalist struggle, that have informed the selection of material included in this brief study. From their experience and intimate knowledge of Namibia, and from the special contribution of other experts on the region, the following analysis has been drawn.

October 1981

1 The Blocking of Namibia's Independence

An Historical Perspective

Occupation

At the time the Dutch East India Company founded its small station at the Cape in 1652, Namibia was occupied by agricultural and pastoral communities of Ovambo, Damara, Herero, Nama and San peoples living far to the north between the Kalahari and Namib deserts. The arrival of missionaries, traders and businessmen during the nineteenth century heralded a colonial scramble between Britain and Germany for the coast of south-west Africa. In an Anglo-German agreement of July 1890, a territory of 318,000 square miles, more than three times the size of Britain, was finally annexed by Germany. Walvis Bay, occupied from Cape Colony decades earlier, remained in British hands. This large region was later named Namibia after its coastal desert.

The colonial exploitation of Namibia might be described as robbery with violence. It met with determined resistance from leaders of African communities. Namibians were in a state of almost continual rebellion from 1904 to 1908. In retaliation for these major uprisings by Herero and Nama people, the Kaiser's forces under von Trotha conducted the first genocide of this century; *Schutztruppen* and concentration camps accounted for the deaths of tens of thousands in extermination campaigns foreshadowing the Nazi massacre of the Jews.

During this first phase of contact with 'white civilisation' large tracts of arable and pasture land were occupied by German colonists, and by British and German companies. The principal goal was mineral wealth; diamonds were discovered in 1908. Effective colonial rule did not extend to the distant north, where most Ovambo-speaking communities were left in relative peace. White settlement occurred mainly in central and southern Namibia, particularly around Windhoek, in

9

areas tellingly known as 'the police zone'. By the outbreak of the First World War, having reduced the Herero population from 70,000 to 16,000 and the Nama from 50,000 to 20,000, the Kaiser's Imperial authorities had handed over much *de facto* control to a settler population of some 15,000 traders, farmers, and missionaries.

The second phase

Namibians entered a second phase of colonial occupation when troops of the Union of South Africa marched into the capital, Windhoek, in May 1915. On 17 December 1920, South Africa was given the mandate of trusteeship for Namibia by the newly formed League of Nations. Smuts and Botha had been trusty members of the British Imperial War Cabinet and Union forces had administered south-west Africa for the past five years. The Union of South Africa was only stopped from simply annexing the territory by United States pressure. Land seized from German settlers and companies was partly granted or sold to South African settlers and companies, and partly returned to Germans, contrary to at least general promises to restore it to Africans. In 1922 the administration of Walvis Bay was returned to South West Africa — the colonial name for Namibia.

Trusteeship meant that South Africa, under a mandate to the British Crown, continued to administer the territory with full legislative powers, supposedly as 'a sacred trust of civilisation'. The League of Nations became the sovereign authority over Namibia with all disputes over interpretation of the mandate referred to the Permanent Court of International Justice. Though annual reports on South Africa's administration had to be submitted to the League's Permanent Mandates Commission, no danger existed of them being effectively challenged by its imperial and colonial members. The mandate, 'to promote to the utmost the material and moral wellbeing and the social progress' of Namibians, was ignored.

The areas of white settlement, (the old German 'police zone'), continued to be administered solely in the settlers' interests with severe restrictions on blacks. In a 1922 Native Administration Proclamation, all Africans living in 'the zone' were confined to reserves and subject to police checks and pass laws. Even when this legislation was denounced by the Mandates Commission and League members, no effective mechanism existed to stop South Africa putting it into force.

Colonial occupation was consolidated between the two world wars. The administration's policies reflected the demands of British dominated mining companies and those of Afrikaner and German farmers and ranchers. Africans' labour and land, the latter reduced from over 80 million hectares to 30 million under the Germans and never restored, were brought under the control of the South African state. The taxation system, drought and coercion by tribal chiefs continued to drive labour from the more densely populated north to distant mines and European farms, a process that had begun around the turn of the century. In 1925 a contract labour system was introduced under a central government agency. In the same year the white settlers were given a degree of political control over the territory in a legislative assembly with an executive committee.

The United Nations

The United Nations, which took the place of the League of Nations in 1945, replaced its Permanent Mandates Commission with a less accommodating Trusteeship Commission. The ex-colonial states, which took their place alongside Liberia and Ethiopia in the General Assembly after the war, were quick to challenge the conduct of the Union government. When Dr Malan's Afrikaner National Party came to power in 1948, annual administrative reports ceased. Dr Malan, with an eye to boosting National Party power through settler votes in South West Africa (SWA), refused to acknowledge the United Nations as the lineal, legal descendant of the League, and made Namibia *de facto* a fifth province of the Republic. Six MPs from South West Africa, always from the National Party and elected by an exclusively white franchise, were seated in the South African parliament; one of them, Mr A.H. du Plessis, was later made a South African cabinet minister. In reply, the International Court of Justice ruled that South Africa could not unilaterally alter the status of Namibia and that the United Nations mandate was still in force, a ruling that had no effect in the territory.

South Africa's coup against the United Nations cleared the way for greater intervention in the political economy of Namibia. Since the late 1940s the territory began to have greater economic significance than during the interwar period, and it was increasingly subordinated to South African economic interests. The 1954 SWA Native Affairs Administration Act placed control of black Namibians directly under the central administration in Pretoria. Henceforth land in Namibia, particularly in the central plateau, was to serve even more as *Lebensraum* for Afrikanerdom. The Odendaal Commission Report of 1964 proposed the extension of a new version of South Africa's homelands policy to Namibia. The foundations of the apartheid groundplan were laid in the 1968-1969 SWA Constitution Act and SWA Affairs Act.*

Meanwhile, in 1966, the General Assembly of the United Nations

---

* In practice the Odendaal plan was overtaken by events and not implemented in the same rigorous way as in South Africa, where it provided a blueprint for Transkei, Bophuthatatswana and Venda.

had terminated South Africa's mandate and called for its complete withdrawal from Namibia. A Council for South West Africa, later called the United Nations Council for Namibia, was created to hold legal and administrative authority for the territory one year later. Security Council Resolutions 276, 283, 284 of 1970 proclaimed the illegality of South Africa's administration of Namibia. This declaration was further supported by a 1971 advisory opinion of the International Court of Justice which upheld the legality of the 1966 revocation of the mandate and the obligation on South Africa, as a result, to withdraw immediately from Namibia. In the court's ruling all member states of the United Nations were called on to acknowledge the illegality of South Africa's occupation and to refrain from all dealings implying recognition. All 'rights' to resources in Namibia purportedly granted by South Africa subsequent to the 1966 mandate revocation were declared void and illegal.

The Rise of Namibian Nationalism

Early resistance
Organised nationalist resistance by Namibians to South Africa's occupation began during the continent-wide upsurge of nationalist sentiment of the late 1950s. This was not, of course, the first resistance to European rule.

The risings against German conquests, a 1922 Nama rebellion in which South Africa pioneered the use of airpower against civilian populations, and Ovambo resistance to South African conquests in the north, are the most prominent examples of Namibians' early readiness to fight back. Nor did the tradition of resistance ever die out: Chief Hosea Kutako of the Herero and the African clergy of the Lutheran Churches kept alive the tradition from which stemmed further reasoned protest and the struggle for political and economic redress. Among the first petitions to the UN Trusteeship Council were ones from Namibians and their representatives like the missionary Rev. Michael Scott. However, prior to the 1950s, this protest was through either traditional or church leaders, and not through modern, mass-based, national political organisations.

Mass organisations
The first of these mass organisations was the Ovamboland Peoples' Organisation (OPO), formed in 1958 by Namibian students and contract workers; open to all Namibians, its primary goal was to work for contract labourers and to fight against racial discrimination. On 19

April 1960, with Sam Nujoma as one of its founding members, it was renamed 'South West Africa Peoples' Organisation' (SWAPO). Reflecting the make-up of Namibia's population, particularly its students and wage-labourers, SWAPO was predominantly recruited from Ovambo-speakers; people from other language groups were members and founding leaders, but were in a minority.

By drawing heavily on the support of its contract workers, SWAPO was able to organise in almost all parts of Namibia, as well as to build up support amongst the northern agricultural communities with the help of its founding president Hermann Toivo Ya Toivo. Namibia's contract labour system had created a group capable of forging a rural-urban alliance against the colonial system.

'Contract', by combining exploitation, denial of common humanity, and physical suffering, had been an educational and consciousness-raising device. Namibian workers came to relate their workplace grievances to the entirety of the apartheid system in Namibia and not simply to particular companies or individuals. Because the labour force at each employment centre was drawn from several communities, with a nationwide scattering of northern contract workers, the labour system created a national consciousness and facilitated SWAPO's organisational efforts. The closed ethnic compounds for Ovambo workers acted as forcing houses for political militants where discontent could readily be expressed in political organisation.* Under Sam Nujoma, a railway worker educated at an Anglican school in Windhoek, who fled in 1960 to avoid arrest and detention, SWAPO was able to build up a number of external offices in Africa and Europe.

At the same time, a more geographically and numerically limited group of Namibians, largely students and people in professions with a dominant proportion of Herero-speakers, developed into the South West Africa National Union (SWANU). The movement had started as an alliance between the Herero Chiefs Council and OPO to protest at population removals around Windhoek; after the withdrawal of the Herero chiefs and OPO's development into SWAPO, the remaining Herero-speakers formed the body of SWANU, lobbying with great success at the OAU and UN. However, despite a strong radical nationalist line, SWANU failed to sustain momentum during the 1970s owing to the lack of a coherent internal organisation. It suffered from a recurrent tendency to become embroiled in intra-Herero parochial politics and lacked real links with African workers and peasants.

Both organisations, like their Zimbabwean counterparts, at first

---

* For example, a Consolidated Diamond Mines executive estimated SWAPO support among the workforce at Oranjemund in 1981 at 90%.

sought a constitutional resolution of their nationalist demands through the official juridical authority over their territory; for Namibians this meant the mandatory power, South Africa, at home, and the United Nations, internationally. However, the United Nations remained rather less than the sum of its parts, having authority but no power. The repeated and continuing refusal of Britain, France and the United States to empower the United Nations to use the sanctions weapon against South Africa, and their failure to bring Namibia to independence by strong diplomatic pressure, has left this situation unchanged. Namibians have been left no other course of action but armed struggle or submission to illegal authority.

In the early 1960s both SWAPO and the churches were committed to operating within the existing political framework in order to change it. They pursued gradualism, reformism and non-violence. They were met on the South African side by different forms of violence: the passive institutionalised violence that denied blacks access to land, education and adequate incomes, and the active violence that left eleven dead in 1959 when police fired on demonstrators who were protesting against the forced clearance of the Windhoek suburb of Pionerspark.

Rejecting the system

Under the impact of South Africa's ruthless pursuit of apartheid segregation, arrests, police harassment and torture, SWAPO and, more slowly, the churches were pushed into a denial of the legitimacy of the existing order, and into a quest for a just society. For SWAPO this meant the use of violence to end the South African illegal occupation. By 1963, SWAPO were training the People's Liberation Army of Namibia, PLAN. They began a guerrilla war after the International Court of Justice had denied the justiciability of a complaint by Liberia and Ethiopia against South Africa's occupation of Namibia. In 1966 a major engagement at Ongulumbashe signalled the beginning of a war in northern Namibia, requiring the South African Defence Forces to take over the region from the police. Three years later, after the notorious Pretoria trials, SWAPO members led by Hermann Toivo Ya Toivo were sentenced to imprisonment on Robben Island under the South African Terrorism Act. Initially a strong opponent of armed struggle, Toivo had been forced by events to accept the moral right of Namibians to use force and had given it his personal endorsement as a last resort.

In the churches comparable agonising decisions had to be taken. They divided Namibia's Christian communities starkly along racial lines. On 28 September 1967, the leaders of the Evangelical Lutheran OvamboKavango Church (ELOC) and the Evangelical Lutheran

Church in South West Africa (ELC) sent a memorandum to the Pretoria government. In it they complained about population removals, rent rises, the denial of rights of free movement and land purchase, and, in the strongest language, about the torture of detainees.

A response by Bishop L. Auala of ELOC and Pastor P. Gowaseb of ELC to the International Court's 1971 advisory opinion represented a turning point for the black churches.* Repeatedly referring to the UN Charter of Human Rights, the two church leaders, in an open letter, firmly denounced the conduct of the South African administration. From this point onwards their churches persistently expressed popular rejection of state violence and moved towards a growing acceptance of the moral right of individuals to oppose it by force. The white Deutsch Evangelisch Lutherische Kirche (DELK) dissociated itself publicly from the statement on the grounds that it was political in intent.

The open letter was a significant factor contributing to a major strike by contract workers at the turn of 1972, an action that Bishop Auala came to support after talking to labourers. This strike was followed by a wave of rural unrest culminating in the declaration of a state of emergency. The missionary leaders of the Anglican Church in Namibia, Bishops Wood and Winter, were deported as they shared and expressed the concerns of the black Lutherans. Increasingly the ecumenical grouping of Anglican and Lutheran black churches took on a role as the voice of the voiceless and champion of human rights in Namibia.

While the Portuguese colonial empire was still intact SWAPO's armed struggle had little chance of immediate success; PLAN could conduct little more than hit-and-run operations and campaigns of rural politicisation. For the majority of Namibians the issue of guerrilla war remained more theoretical than practical. The demise of the Portuguese government under the weight of its colonial wars in April 1974 opened a new chapter for southern Africa.

Despite attempts by Pretoria to stem the radical nationalist tide by imposing a UNITA regime in Angola favourable to South Africa, independence was declared in Luanda under an MPLA government willing to support SWAPO, even at heavy cost. In response to ill-judged covert intervention in Angola by the United States in support of the UNITA troops, overtly backed by South African invasion forces, MPLA called on the assistance of Cuban troops. The future of Namibia had suddenly taken on regional and international dimensions.

* See Appendix F.

SWAPO was now able to establish bases near the Angolan border and to intensify its guerrilla war. The issue of armed struggle was no longer distant and many Namibian Christians made up their minds. Young people fled in their thousands to join PLAN. The apartheid brought to Namibia by South Africa had made the black churches part of the resistance movement; chaplains were assigned to refugee camps by the Anglican and Lutheran Churches. South Africa had a major colonial war on its hands.

Background to South Africa's Internal Settlement

The destruction of an economy

Apartheid has never meant parallel or dual economies but division of labour within a unity of exploitation. South West Africa's apartheid was no exception. The pre-colonial economies based on agriculture were in effect destroyed. African production of food and shelter, the basis of life for most households, today amounts at most to 4% of the territory's gross production. This compares with a range of 15-25% in sub-Saharan Africa. So-called 'subsistence' households cannot in fact survive on their own production alone; even staple grain harvests fall short of minimum requirements.

What remains is no fossilised pre-colonial remnant but a disintegrating caricature of African societies with their directions of change shaped over eight decades by, and in the interests of, successive colonial powers. The 'failure' of the traditional economy to adapt and develop was imposed: land theft denied it the space, lack of education denied it the expertise, controls and limitations cut it off from market opportunities, migrant labour on low wages denied it access to finance and drained it of adult manpower as well as leading directly to massive family and social disintegration.

The 'reserves', 'homelands', 'Bantustans' — the titles have changed — were 'developed' by Europeans to create a labour reserve economy. They kept 'unnecessary' dependents and unemployed would-be workers out of the 'white' towns and farms. By providing a portion of the subsistence needs of dependents and unemployed, they allowed the payment of wages below the family subsistence level without destroying the labour force. The system would not have survived were workers' families resident near their workplaces and totally dependent on wage incomes.

This labour reserve system is probably no longer in the direct economic interest of the mining and large-scale service sectors. Their requirements for a stable, skilled and reasonably content labour force are not, and cannot be, met within its parameters, as the shrewder of the transnationals like Anglo-American have recognised for at least a decade. However the European ranching and seasonal processing industries retain their old interests; they are still dependent on low wages to sustain the standard of living of their white proprietors.

Historically the labour reserve system was important to the three key sectors of Namibian industry, mining, fishing and stock-rearing. Until the late 1940s none of these sectors was able to survive on its own revenues even with sub-subsistence wages paid to its workers. The increase in state subsidies needed to support settlers, administration and companies in a free labour market would not have been practicable for the, then, weak South African economy.

A model colony

Hopes that the exploitation of Namibia's land, labour and resources would produce surpluses had to be deferred until after the Second World War. From the late 1950s to the late 1970s, the territory's gross production rose on average 6% per annum, almost entirely due to the growth of mining and fishing. Remittances to South Africa amounted to about one-third of the value of this national production. South Africa's own exports to Namibia amounted to over 400 million Rand by the end of the 1970s. In consequence the colonial economy brought growing amounts of hard currency and surplus to the Republic's economy as well as to particular settler, civil service and business groups inside Namibia and to their non-South African transnational partners. In the mid-1970s Namibia's budget was in full balance with receipts covering capital as well as recurrent expenditure — this included massive subsidies to settlers. In colonial economic terms, as seen by the colonising power, Namibia was a modern model colony. Mr Vorster had good reason to wish to sustain such a profitable relationship.

After the International Court's 1971 opinion, non-aligned countries began to exert pressure on the west in the United Nations for sanctions on South Africa. The casuistry required from the west to justify its refusal was embarrassing and entailed diplomatic costs in relations with African states that rose annually. This was not lost on Pretoria. Prime Minister Vorster, who saw his defensive 'independent' homelands policy as the necessary extension of the apartheid groundplan in South Africa, now applied this logic to Namibia: homelands had to be given the trappings of 'self-government' leading to 'independence'. The interests of white South Africa, the mining companies, and the now 110,000 resident whites* — civil servants, farmers and miners — could be guaranteed by limiting black political

---

* Perhaps 55,000 settlers and 55,000 contract expatriates with homes in South Africa.

rights to ethnic councils. The goal was the balkanisation of Namibia with the bulk of the territory and almost all the natural resources and capital stock in the 'white ethnic unit'. A first step would be a national advisory council, under white rule, with representatives from all ethnic groups to create a constitution for this dismemberment. These proposals were communicated to a United Nations envoy in 1972.

There was, however, every reason not to hurry towards such a 'solution'. Firstly, the economic benefits of profit and savings remittances to South Africa, and of Namibian purchases from the Republic, would be harder to safeguard under a neo-colonial settlement. South Africa, which is not a fully-fledged industrial economy, would face stronger outside competition in a neo-colonial dispensation than it did under its colonial relationship with Namibia. Furthermore the plan might not succeed; it was unlikely that Namibians, and international opinion, would accept without resistance only a town-council and tribal level of political representation for blacks.

The scheme was essentially a contingency plan, in case the military, financial, economic and diplomatic costs of the war and South Africa's illegal occupation rose too high. The mere discussion of the scheme would in itself serve to sustain the illusion that South Africa was 'seeking a solution to the Namibia problem' and, so help to buy time for an internal settlement. Its implementation was evoked by the consequences of the April 1974 coup in Portugal.

The Turnhalle Conference

In a flurry of activity, six months after the coup, when rapid independence for Portugal's African colonies under radical governments became certain, Mr Vorster declared that South West Africa must determine its own future. The echoes quickly returned from his National Party colleagues in Namibia: Mr A.H. du Plessis announced that a constitutional conference would take place; Mr Dirk Mudge stressed that only tribal authorities, not political parties, would be permitted to participate. A few weeks later, key Zimbabwean nationalists were released from jail; Rhodesia was to have a constitutional conference too, under Bishop Muzorewa's umbrella.

These attempts to forge stable buffer states around South Africa represented the defensive face of 'détente', and a partial coming together of United States and South African interests in the region. In the wake of OPEC price rises, the United States was becoming increasingly aware of the strategic significance of southern Africa's mineral resources. The region, with its deposits of gold, diamonds, coal, copper, uranium, chrome, vanadium and manganese, took on a sudden importance in the last two years of Dr Kissinger's secretaryship of state. The inherent instability of the countries in which they were mined became a problem, graphically illustrated by the Cuban presence and eastern bloc support for liberation movements, requiring a more active western interest and intervention in the region.

For the EEC countries, particularly Britain and France, and to a lesser degree West Germany, the interest was always there; southern Africa was a major theatre for trade, profit and diplomacy. However inaccurate the strategic arithmetic of the world's mineral resources — for the USA and Britain are not as dependent on South Africa's minerals as they seem to believe, or, at least, as they sometimes like to pretend — southern Africa was moving up the west's agenda from 'any other business' to a secondary but priority area.

The old German *Turnhalle* or gymnasium building served as the venue in Windhoek for Mr Vorster's constitutional conference. With a white secretariat to control proceedings, a motley gathering of largely South African-selected tribal delegates began meeting on 1 September 1975. There were 16 delegates from the unpopular quisling Ovambo authority, supposedly representing 46% of the population. The Damara Advisory Council had refused to attend, so the South African-sponsored political party, the Damara United Front (DUF), produced 30 delegates despite the ban on other parties like SWAPO and SWANU. The traditional Nama leadership also refused and Nama appointees of South Africa appeared. Chief Clemens Kapuuo, representing at best a fraction of the deeply divided Herero community, led 40 delegates. A variety of delegations 'represented' other communities.

A Declaration of Intent appeared under Mr Dirk Mudge's direction two weeks later: ethnic representation at a tribal level; overarching *de facto* white national government with its dominant ethnic unit, the European, capable of vetoing all decisions; Bantustan-style regionalism in rural areas and, in theory, multiple ethnic enclaves in urban areas. The UN Security Council responded to this glaringly unrepresentative conference with Resolution 385 calling for free and universal non-ethnic elections under United Nations control.

Pressures for change

The constitution that finally emerged from the Turnhalle Conference in March 1977 was plainly a Frankenstein monster and the west would not accept it. A council of eleven ministers, each from an ethnic group, was to rule Namibia, none with a specific portfolio and jointly served by a secretary to the cabinet who was head of an all-white civil service. Ethnic governments with responsibility for education, housing and health, each with their own bureaucracy, would be elected by means chosen by themselves; they would have the right to reverse decisions made by their delegates in the central parliament.* Supreme power, subject to veto by any ethnic group, would lie with the central legislature which alone had responsibility for defence and foreign affairs; a Supreme Court was limited to advisory functions. It was unworkable and the South Africans probably knew it.

Yet the Turnhalle constitution might have immediately taken on life outside the laboured verbal gymnastics of its authors, but for three unrelated events outside Namibia: the failure of the 1975 South African invasion of Angola, the South African 1976 urban uprisings, and the American elections of that year. The state terrorism with which the risings were quelled touched the memories of American blacks and horrified the business world. Powerful transnational corporations thought twice about the competence of the Vorster government to create internal and regional stability. Dr Kissinger, in another bout of shuttle diplomacy, left no doubt as to American concern about events in the region. Early in 1977 a Contact Group made up of Britain, France, and the USA, plus the two elected North Atlantic members of the Security Council, Canada and West Germany, was formed to mediate in negotiations for an implementation of UN resolutions on Namibia.

The human rights emphasis of the new Carter administration in the USA, and mounting European alarm at the growing instability of the southern Africa region, gave some momentum to the Contact Group initiative. The American ambassador to the United Nations, Andrew Young, shared the liberal goals of the British foreign secretary, Dr David Owen, and provided a cutting edge to the Contact Group. Their initial aim was to create a compromise on Resolution 385, to get SWAPO involved in an election with UN observers but without a total withdrawal of South African forces. This meant putting pressure on Pretoria at a time when contempt for the pusillanimity of the west over the CIA fiasco in Angola was high. Yet never before had South Africa been more of a pariah in international eyes and in more need of western support.

The Turnhalle constitution, designed to create an interim government, now needed urgent cosmetic changes and efforts to make it less impracticable. It was remodelled around its principal design features: three-tier government, a first tier made up of a multi-ethnic pseudo-cabinet and legislature with provisions allowing *de facto* white con-

---

* Namibians already had experience of elections to homeland administrations. After only a 2.5% turnout in 1973, homelands functionaries, tribal authorities and police manipulated the vote in 1975 by intimidation and bribery. The administrations were not strictly regional in that, theoretically, they had power over members of their ethnic group wherever they resided; this was nominal with respect to white mining, ranching and urban areas.

trol, and a second and third regional and urban ethnic tier allowing white towns to stay under white municipal councils. The Turnhalle representatives reformed as a Democratic Turnhalle Alliance (DTA); a minority, including representatives of the bulk of the European community, broke away to form the Action Front for the Preservation of the Turnhalle Principles (AKTUR). The latter were committed to a rigid and provocative interpretation of the Odendaal plan shared by the majority of the white community.

The Contact Group came away from its 1977 negotiations with South Africa with the understanding that the interim period before the implementation of the UN proposals would see a South African Administrator-General working closely with a representative of the UN Secretary-General to bring Namibia to independence. But the idea that the 'scrapping' of the Turnhalle constitution and the appointment of the Administrator-General represented a basic change in South African goals or tactics was wishful thinking. The purpose of the Administrator-General, as subsequent events revealed, was to articulate and implement speedily some version of the internal settlement formula soon to be tried in Rhodesia. His role was to provide enough appearance of movement to keep international pressures at bay and to reduce demands for substantive change; failing that prevarication and more blatant moves to wreck negotiations were available.

Western attitudes

After the creation of the Contact Group, there was no doubt that western diplomacy would play its part in bringing Namibia to independence. The unresolved issues were what kind of independence, when, and after what type of transition, difficult questions for nations preoccupied with United Nations and eastern bloc support for SWAPO. The immediate question in dispute was whether the initial Turnhalle internal settlement formula, which excluded majority black political parties, or one incorporating them as subordinate partners in coalition governments, would work internally and be accepted internationally. As to the coalition option, 'white government with black faces', Britain judged that in Rhodesia it was worth exploring, but that in Namibia it would fail owing to different circumstances, notably the complete absence of a black middle class and of any black leaders with previous nationalist credentials to lend plausibility to the coalition.

South Africa was adamant that this formula had to be made to work; time had to be found, and the necessary basis for DTA rule built up. The west was no less aware that unless SWAPO were involved in this 'national solution' it would founder on internal resistance and international protest. The product of these conflicting emphases was over four years of inconclusive negotiations. These gave South Africa time to attempt to consolidate the position of the DTA and the west a tactical excuse — however morally inadequate — to veto UN resolutions calling for sanctions, and to ignore the decrees of the UN Council for Namibia.

Three years earlier, the UN Council for Namibia had issued a decree pursuant to the 1971 International Court advisory opinion; it claimed authority over all mineral exploitation in the territory with provisions for forfeiture for parties contravening the decree.* All companies or agencies extracting and exporting Namibia's mineral wealth thereafter did so in contravention of a decree by a duly constituted *de jure* administration of Namibia.** They ran the risk, admittedly so far theoretical, of their cargoes being impounded, or of damages being due to a future legal government of Namibia.

However, Britain, under both Conservative and Labour governments, has persisted in honouring illegal contracts to buy uranium from the Rössing mine in Namibia. Rössing is the largest uranium mine in the world and represents a massive capital investment by RTZ (formerly the Rio Tinto Zinc Corporation), its major equity participant. The last Labour government, while acknowledging that the transactions were 'unlawful', allowed them to continue, and the situation remains unchanged under the foreign secretaryship of Lord Carrington.† Britain, West Germany, France, Netherlands, Switzerland, USSR, and Japan, the countries buying uranium oxide from Rössing, facilitating its indirect sale, or selling enrichment plant services for purchasers, appear to hold the International Court's 1971 opinion on Namibia in contempt. There can be little doubt that this wide international participation in the removal of Namibia's mineral resources via illegal contracts casts a question mark over the impartiality of the Contact Group in SWAPO's eyes.

The basic contracts for Rössing were concluded under the Wilson government in Britain during 1967-1969, *after* the revocation of South Africa's mandate. They might be characterised as a major achievement by South Africa, RTZ and the British energy ministry under Mr Anthony Wedgwood Benn. For the first two the contracts were critical, though for different reasons: to South Africa to allow it to obtain geo-political involvement in, and commitment to, the colonial political economy in Namibia by a major transnational and a major western power; to RTZ to enable it to open up a major new source of

---

* The decree was approved by the General Assembly on 13 December 1974.

** See the BCC statement in Appendix C.

† Lord Carrington was a director of RTZ from 1974-1979.

profit and reinforce RTZ's position in the expanding global uranium oxide industry. It was presumably valuable also to the British Department of Energy, which obtained a low-cost source of fuel for its atomic electricity generating programme. South Africa's and RTZ's objectives have been met. However, given RTZ's successful renegotiation of prices to Britain, the world glut of uranium and the impact the Rössing contracts have had on Namibian attitudes to the United Kingdom, it is less clear that the interests of Britain have been equally well served.

The Democratic Turnhalle Alliance (DTA)

On 1 September 1977, a South African Administrator-General (AG), Mr Justice M.T. Steyn, took office in Namibia. He was effectively a governor of a South African colony charged with achieving political and military decolonisation while sustaining the colony's dependent economic relations in a new neo-colonial relationship. Just how this was to be achieved was certainly not worked out in fine detail, nor, probably, was there any consensus about its immediate desirability. Under pressure South Africa was to blunder from one untenable position to another, propelled by the momentum of events as much as shaping them.

The new South African strategy

Pressure on South Africa from the Contact Group, led by David Owen and Andrew Young, was growing by mid-1978. Rhodesia's internal settlement was showing little promise and the National Party in South Africa, weakened by the 'Muldergate' Information scandal, was on the defensive. As a precaution the administration of the vital town and port of Walvis Bay was removed from Namibia and placed under the jurisdiction of Cape Province in South Africa. The legal process of reclaiming Walvis Bay from South West Africa had tellingly begun on the day that Administrator-General Steyn was appointed. Pretoria at first appeared to accept western proposals but then refused to negotiate with SWAPO, attempting to forestall agreement by launching a savage raid into southern Angola.

On 4 May 1978 South African troops destroyed a large refugee camp at Kassinga, killing some 750 Namibians, mostly non-combatants, a majority of them children and students. About 270 people were taken captive back to Namibia; after interrogation, frequently accompanied by torture, less than 160 were released. The remaining 112 are still detained in a concentration camp at the Tenegab military base near Mariental. The massacre had the desired result of gaining Mr Vorster support in South Africa, but failed to stop

SWAPO accepting the UN proposals worked out by the Contact Group two months later.

The Kassinga raid heralded a new military strategy throughout southern Africa of 'pre-emptive strikes', a sustained attempt to destroy the transport systems and economic infrastructure of front-line states harbouring guerrillas. Incorporated, sometimes subliminally, sometimes more overtly, in Pretoria's bid for a constellation of states to establish South Africa's economic power more fully over the region, was a military claim to a right to operate within the borders of neighbouring states in pursuit of the same 'total strategy'. Military preparations to 'take the war to the enemy' were packaged in humble appeals for the need of 'hot pursuit' or disarming offers to defend 'constellation' regimes against their external and internal enemies.

On 6 August 1978, Mr Martti Ahtisaari, UN Commissioner for Namibia, arrived in Windhoek with a large team to a huge and joyous airport crowd of blacks. A settlement seemed at hand. However, the South Africans were insisting on an impossibly rapid schedule for elections in under four months that would not permit adequate UN supervision. After long and abortive negotiations — ominously, registration of voters under South African control had begun some three months earlier — the Administrator-General simply announced that purely internal elections would go ahead in December without UN supervision. Nine days later, the plan for implementing a ceasefire and UN supervised elections was adopted by the Security Council as Resolution 435. The United Nations had been cynically out-manoeuvred by the South African government.

This dramatic revelation of South Africa's real intentions came during the transition from the Vorster to P.W. Botha governments in the Republic and the abruptness of the apparent volte-face might be attributed to it. The future of Namibia, as far as the new South African Prime Minister was concerned, was to be determined by two major factors: considerations of total strategy in relation to the defence of the Republic, and the struggle within the National Party between the advocates of different ways of retaining apartheid and white supremacy. When the foreign ministers of the Contact Group countries, in full diplomatic disarray, met the new South African administration, General Magnus Malan was seated at the right hand of Mr P.W. Botha. Together they had borne the brunt of the Angola humiliation; together they were resolved to avoid becoming 'the men who lost Namibia'. The Contact Group left Pretoria in October 1978 after a total diplomatic failure.

'Responsible self-government'

The December 1978 internal elections in Namibia were marked by enforced registration, bribery, intimidation and electoral fraud on a massive scale. SWAPO and a number of other smaller non-ethnic parties refused to take part; even the white Federal Party declined. Government support for the DTA and the conduct of the elections represented a travesty of democratic procedures; the lowest common denominator of western supporters of the DTA was the insulting claim that nothing better could be expected of elections in Africa. The elections were roundly denounced as a sham by Namibia's church leaders and the extent of the fraud graphically illustrated in a CIIR/BCC publication *Elections in Namibia?*, written by the ex-secretary of the ecumenical Christian Centre in Windhoek, Justin Ellis.

The election results gave the DTA 41 of the 50 seats in a new Constituent Assembly. AKTUR took only 6 seats, though the majority of the white votes. Each of the three minor parties took one of the remaining seats. The interim government plan, shelved in 1976, was coming into being as 'responsible self-government for Namibia'.

The west's hesitant verdict that the DTA was doomed required that South Africa set about creating two new groups to reassure the world of the DTA's viability. A black elite who might equate their interests with such a dispensation rather than with the goals of radical populist and/or socialist nationalists in SWAPO was one group. A black-manned, white-led South West African army, home guard and police force to defend the state was the other. Such Namibians with a stake in the neo-colonial political economy might provide a support for, and complement, the largely discredited tribal leadership of the DTA. At worst, they would moderate the pressures from a future SWAPO government for any radical transformation of the Namibian economy.

Concessions and repression
Time was needed for this strategy. Inducements had to be provided to the new elite and to their wavering supporters in the west, while steps were taken to contain the impact of SWAPO political organisers, guerrillas and nationalist church leaders. Within a period of four years, school teachers' salaries rose dramatically and promotions became easier; refresher courses were introduced and technical colleges were built.

Such projects were able to elicit the aid of anxious mining companies and commercial interests in Namibia. A Private Sector Foundation, similar in goals to the South African Urban Foundation, was formed. Its aim was to improve 'the quality of life' of urban blacks; it promoted black home ownership in concert with the Windhoek municipality, and, headed by Dr Z. Ngavirue, it drew on funds from mining companies and commerce.

At Rössing, renowned then for its poor worker conditions, considerable improvements were made, particularly in wages. A handful of black white-collar workers were allowed to move into the white Swakopmund suburb of Veneta; and at the Arandis township near the mine a carefully graded mixing of black and 'Coloured' workers was permitted. A Rössing Foundation now offers a handful of scholarships, runs an adult education centre and provides a limited amount of money for charitable efforts towards black advancement.

Consolidated Diamond Mines, benefiting from an enormous and unexpected rise in diamond prices in the late 1970s, has gone further with integrated school, health and recreational facilities, provision of leave transport for its contract employees, a start towards family housing for a portion of its African employees and finance for a large technical college at Ongwediva in the north. The transnationals applauded the removal of the South African Mixed Marriages and Immorality Act and the repeal of most petty apartheid legislation — in some cases, discrimination became a criminal offence — provisions that have remained a dead-letter owing to white opposition.

This coming together of the interests of some elements in the private sector with the administration paralleled developments in the Republic. The goal of this sudden interest in black advancement was to create a small elite capable of ensuring the stability of the foreign-dominated and export-oriented economy of Namibia. The total strategy theories of General Magnus Malan, coming out of the counter-insurgency classrooms of the United States' military academies, were finding a dusty laboratory in the territory. Its themes were part of an evolution of apartheid towards a National Security State.*

Attempts were made to foster splits in SWAPO while SWANU and SWAPO dissidents were courted and brought back to prominence in Namibia. New legislation had already put the strategy into practice. The 1967 South African Terrorism Act was retained while new 'security' laws were introduced. Proclamation AG9 (1977) was presented as part of a 'liberalisation'; periods of detention incommunicado were reduced to 96 hours and some meetings were permitted in the north in theory, once permission had been obtained. However, by 1979, AG9 had been changed to allow repeated detention under renewable 30-day orders without recourse to legal counsel, within the framework of a wider martial law proclamation for the north introducing a curfew after which individuals could be shot on sight. AG26 allowed the Administrator-General to detain pre-emptively anyone thought likely

---

* See CIIR's *South Africa in the 1980s* published 1980, and Appendix D.

to be a threat to law and order. In similar fashion the repeal of pass laws and residence restrictions was promptly followed by anti-vagrancy legislation quite openly stated to serve the same purpose.

Over forty of the SWAPO leadership were detained in the wake of the murder of Chief Clemens Kapuuo — probably killed as a result of intra-DTA Herero jealousies quite unconnected with SWAPO. Gobabis prison was converted into a detention centre. Repression was kept as hidden as possible from the mass media while 'liberalisation' was presented as the DTA's programme and its black elite pushed forward into the limelight. The poorer cousins of this elite were to remain the unseen impoverished inhabitants of the rural areas and urban slums, or internationally trumpeted recruits for the 20,000 strong 'Namibian' army that South Africa set about creating without delay. For some it was a logical continuation of the contract labour system: join the army or starve.

The sinking ship

But alongside repressive legislation designed to curb SWAPO, it was perceived that pressure from Namibian workers could no longer be safely totally suppressed. New union legislation consistent with some of the recommendations of the Wiehahn Commission in the Republic was introduced to control the evolution of the trades unions. Strikes like that at Rössing in December 1978 and at Oranjemund in April 1979, and SWAPO's strong roots amongst workers made legal black unions a lesser evil, if under strict government or employer control. However, the only black union to be recognised since 1978 has been the SWA Building Workers' Union, a highly bureaucratic craft union dominated by DTA politicians with a predominantly 'Coloured' membership.

The National Union of Namibian Workers (NUNW), with strong SWAPO membership, had its leaders banned, detained or harassed. The NUNW organiser at Rössing, Arthur Pickering, was driven into exile after a series of arrests and suppressed strikes. The most tenacious surveyor and publicist of labour conditions, Pastor Gerson Max, has frequently been detained or confined to his house. As with their equivalents in South Africa, the Namibian labour 'reforms' are unworkable as registration implies for many workers that the union has begun collaborating with the employer rather than expressing their grievances effectively.

The appointment in 1979 of Dr G. Viljoen, chairman of the Afrikaner elite's Broederbond society and usually seen as one of South Africa's most powerful men, marked a sharp upgrading of the post of Administrator-General and the quest for a viable basis to a 'national solution'. His two chief goals were to recruit plausible black faces for the DTA and rebuild a unified white position through his Broederbond connections. On both counts he failed.

He had high hopes of Andreas Shipanga, a dissident founding member of SWAPO who formed a self-styled SWAPO(D) — (D) standing for democratic. However Shipanga declined to board what he saw as an unpopular and sinking ship. Viljoen's flirtation with a 'third force', the Namibia National Front, sponsored by the white professional-based Federal Party with SWANU providing the key members, foundered for similar reasons. Meanwhile white factionalism steadily worsened. The right wing Herstigte Nasionale Party (HNP) cut into AKTUR and DTA support; the Federal Party and Christian Democrat Party shared a middle ground in which concessions were advocated, in favour of mining and professional groups by the former, small business and less conservative German farmers by the latter.

Towards undeclared UDI

In the DTA-dominated Constituent Assembly the South African government had created a new 'fact'. The DTA increasingly developed its own fragmented and somewhat paranoid personality fearful of South African intentions. But its existence permitted an elaborate game of advising and consulting to go on between Windhoek and Pretoria. In a much repeated ventriloquist's act, Mr P.W. Botha was able to speak through the Assembly in an attempt to divert international pressures to Windhoek. These began to grow as intimations that Britain might consider not vetoing sanctions were heard from a frustrated Dr Owen; an abortive meeting attempted in Geneva, in November 1979, between SWAPO, South Africa and the 'internal parties', did little to mend deteriorating relations with the west.

The negotiations that led up to the Geneva meeting established a pattern: a sticking point would be introduced by South Africa, this would be resolved by concessions from SWAPO or the United Nations, but action would be taken by South Africa to break off negotiations. The first point was the size of the UN military presence during transition, the UN Transition Assistance Group (UNTAG). The second was the placement, number and size of SWAPO bases in Namibia after a ceasefire. Negotiations were broken off by March 1979 and major South African raids into Angola took place. Some degree of agreement was now apparently reached through a joint Angolan-Zambian initiative involving Andrew Young; the idea of a Demilitarised Zone (DMZ) was introduced and accepted by SWAPO and South Africa, though no understanding was achieved on the disposition of different forces in this zone.*

During these negotiations the Constituent Assembly was upgraded to a 'National Assembly'. In May 1980 a first tier of the internal settlement superstructure was put in place with a creation of an AG's 'council of ministers'. Its twelve members were nominated by a chairman who was himself elected by the National Assembly. The council took over the territorial powers of the all-white Legislative Assembly and its executive committee, which remained as the second-tier white authority, inconveniently under AKTUR control; its structure ensured DTA rule under Mr Dirk Mudge's chairmanship. A division of 'interstate relations', a potential foreign office, was next set up. Like ten other 'directorates', it was to become a department of a Namibian civil service, temporarily answerable to Pretoria but potentially part of an 'independent' government.

The momentum of South Africa's drive for a 'national solution' showed no sign of slackening in Namibia but faith in its ultimate viability was vanishing fast. The sweeping ZANU (PF) victory in the Zimbabwean elections came as a rude awakening to Pretoria. Not only had the most potentially successful trial of the internal settlement formula failed utterly, despite high levels of South African financial and military aid, it had done so despite considerable British Conservative support. No comparable external help could be expected for the DTA, nor was a white farmer, Dirk Mudge, as negotiable internationally as the black bishop in Zimbabwe. Meanwhile Peter Kalangula, ex-Anglican leader of a small sect and chairman of the Ovambo Executive Council, took over from Pastor Cornelius Ndjoba as chairman of the DTA. He was backed by Katuutire Kaura and Kuaimo Riruako — whose commitment to DTA left much to be desired — representing a group of Herero speakers.

Playing for time

The DTA's extraordinary weakness was demonstrated in second-tier elections held in November 1980 for seats in the ethnic legislative assemblies (effectively the old homelands governments). The only contested election won by the DTA was that of the 'Coloureds' and that by a fairly narrow margin with 40% abstentions. The DTA lost the crucial Damara Legislative Assembly and, as the Republican Party in the whites-only legislature, lost to the National Party by 11 seats to 18. Ovambos were not allowed to vote, ostensibly because of the war, in reality for fear of massive abstentions. The superstructure of the in-

---

* South Africa may have assumed SWAPO would reject the DMZ and accepted it on these incorrect grounds. It was later rejected in June 1981 by both South Africa and the DTA.

ternal settlement was now in place; the problem was that its base lay in Pretoria, not amongst the Namibian electorate.

At the end of 1980 South Africa was looking for time, not so much to make its 'national solution' stick, but to pull out of Namibia at minimal cost. There was no longer any doubt in the minds of either European governments or the South African administration that SWAPO would win in any free UN-supervised elections. Major-General Jannie Geldenhuys, Commander of the South African Defence Forces (SADF) in Namibia, made it clear, in a series of inspired leaks, that he believed that the war was unwinnable, a quick settlement desirable and the 'boys' should be brought home fast to fight 'communism' in the Republic. He, and Dr G. Viljoen whose views seem to have been similar, a no-win position, were rapidly promoted out of Namibia.

A new 'South West Africa Defence Force' was now placed directly under the authority of the Administrator-General, as were the SADF of which it was a 'part'. A 'SWA Police Force' was also formed. They were not only to fight South Africa's colonial war but might complicate UN provisions for the return to base of South African troops during a UN-supervised election. The chairman of the council of ministers would have a voice in the deployment of these troops, doubtless to the same effect as Ian Smith's deployment of Rhodesian forces after Lancaster House.

The new AG, Mr Danie Hough, a relatively junior and obscure administrative officer, looked and behaved like a caretaker. The military and civilian machinery set up under him gave South Africa control of the war, and of interim negotiations with other states. On 14 September 1981 responsibility for running Namibia on a day-to-day basis was handed over to the council of ministers. Namibia was on the brink of 'independence'. But if this step were to be taken in flagrant contempt of international opinion, a public relations exercise and propaganda battle of considerable magnitude had to be waged and won.*

But there was a terrible flaw in Namibia's undeclared UDI. An 'independent' Namibia under DTA rule could only be kept in being by a continued massive presence of South African troops. This would be no less true in the 1980s than it had been in the late 1970s. South Africa's 'national solution' in Namibia, expensive and stillborn, was no solution at all.

---

* One of the latest weapons in the battle is the magazine *Namibia in Focus*, launched by the Windhoek administration's 'Namibia Information Service' from London in July 1981.

2 Namibia Today

A Political Economy of Theft

Population

Namibia's population today is usually estimated by unreliable projections from dubious colonial censuses; from employment data, with adjustments, it stands in late 1981 between 1,460,000 and 1,480,000. Of these perhaps some 90,000 are troops of the South African occupation forces. Some 1,170,000 Africans, 120,000 'Coloureds' (including Nama people), and 110,000 Europeans live in the territory, though about half of the latter would describe themselves as South Africans rather than as *suidwesters*.

Almost one third of this population lives in towns — the numbers are growing because of the war — and the rest are sparsely scattered throughout central and southern Namibia, with a dense community of small-scale African farmers in the north. In addition perhaps 70,000 Namibians, predominantly but not exclusively Africans, are refugees mainly in Angola and Zambia.

Wages

Resident whites in 1977 were earning on average 3,000 Rand per annum.* This average consists mostly of the salaries of businessmen, farmers, a few top managers, and state functionaries plus the income of other skilled white personnel. The average wage for black Namibians was R125 per annum.**

Half the black labour force, some 250,000 people, are engaged in

---

* Figures in this section will be for 1977; white earnings today after inflation and wage increases would be R4,700.
** Comparable increases for blacks were limited to the mining sector, teachers and the rest of the black elite. 'Black' here includes 'Coloureds' and Africans.

31

'subsistence' agriculture with incomes estimated at less than R30 per annum. Of the rest, the majority comprises 75,000 domestic workers earning in 1977 between R125 and R200, and 50,000 labourers on white farms and ranches earning R250-R400, including rudimentary housing and food. The manufacturing and construction industries, with public utilities, account for less than 25,000 black workers. Only in the mining industry, employing some 20,000 blacks, did average incomes exceed R1,500, half the European average, with some skilled workers earning R2,800-R3,000.

Within the Namibian context the mines have a relatively privileged labour force compared with the sub-Poverty Datum Line wages paid in other sectors of the economy, particularly agriculture and domestic service. The Tsumeb copper mine, for example, today has some 6,000 workers the majority of whom earn R3.47-R4.00 per day. Senior miners, about nine to 10 men, earn between R5.20-R9.92 per day. Amongst the smelters, cookers earn R5 for an eight-hour day, while about 10 foremen will get R6.72 per day. However, this is a relative privilege indeed. Some 4,000 workers are crowded in a compound with nothing in the way of facilities and the local hospital, observers in 1981 noted, appeared to lack doctors at the time of their visit. Wages at Rössing and Oranjemund are higher, bringing the average mining wage above R1,500.

Land distribution

The overall picture in Namibia is therefore one of stark wage inequality, a dramatic 20/25 to 1 against 15/16 to 1 even in South Africa and colonial Rhodesia. This racial divide is mirrored in the distribution of Namibia's natural resources. Only 2% of Namibia's 83 million hectares is suitable for crop cultivation, and over half the land is desert. But, as a group, Namibia's 110,000 whites, though mostly landless state functionaries, have possession of 38 million hectares of the best agricultural and ranching land, plus the area containing the country's extensive and varied mineral resources.

Namibia's 1,290,000 blacks have been left 33 million hectares of 'habitable' land, largely arid and sandy soils unsuitable for cultivation. The 'Ovambo homeland' contains an estimated population of 400,000 but less than 50% of its 10 million hectares is suitable for crop cultivation or ranching. The good ranching country of the central plateau, indeed 90% of land outside the northern region, is in Europeans' hands, with 60% of the country's 3 million cattle also owned by whites.

The confiscation of land after conquest during the colonial period, vividly recalled by Herero-speaking people in their demands for the return of their 'lost valleys' taken in 1907, lies at the root of

Namibia's political economy and its people's political consciousness. Contemporary land distribution makes overgrazing and soil erosion inevitable. Overcrowded reserves, in which blacks were until recently forced by legislation to live, make it impossible for Africans to subsist on the land. Today as much as in the past they are pushed by rural poverty into the contract labour system.

A caricature of an economy

The pitiful wages still paid to the majority of workers are scarcely adequate for individuals let alone the households whose major source of income they are. No free market in labour exists today. Employers are in principle, and sometimes in practice, subject to heavy fines for taking on workers who have not registered in the state labour bureaux. Despite enabling legislation, probably directed at international opinion by the DTA, no unions with strong shop-floor organisation have been permitted. Rössing has in-company unions. The Tsumeb corporation has entered into closed-shop agreements with all-white unions which have recently accepted a limited number of blacks. Only at Oranjemund has the management allowed a workers' committee which it believes to be associated with the National Union of Namibian Workers. There are, of course, no unions for domestic and agricultural workers.

Black contract labour was the basis of the major industries which created Namibia's wealth: mining, stock-rearing and, to a lesser extent, fishing, canning and processing. These industries today represent two-thirds of the productive output of the country. They are almost totally export-oriented. The mining of uranium ore, diamonds, copper and lead accounts for one-half, in value, of Namibian production; the net operating surplus, profit, from mining rose from R97.2 million in 1975 to R454.6 million by the end of 1979.* This major mining sector is owned either by South African and other transnational corporations, or by combinations of South African state corporations like IDC with the transnationals. The Rössing mine, for example, amongst other equity participants, has a 46.5% holding by RTZ, 13.2% by IDC and 6.5% by the General Mining and Finance Corporation of South Africa.

This foreign domination of the major productive areas of Namibia's economy has produced a caricature of other colonial economies with a maximisation of profits for repatriation to South Africa or to the headquarters of the transnationals. Some 30% of GDP (Gross Domestic Product, which measures the value of a country's economic production) leaves Namibia as the profits of the major

---

* Wages of *all* employees rose from R52.5 to R106.1 million in the same period.

firms like De Beers, General Mining, RTZ and Amax-Newmont (Tsumeb). De Beers' Oranjemund diamond mines, run by Consolidated Diamond Mines (CDM), alone account for some 10% of GDP annually sent out of the country. In all, over 60% of GDP — a staggering figure — is appropriated as company profits before tax. The subsidiary industries that might be expected to arise are often to be found in South Africa or abroad: diamond sorting and valuing, further refining of copper, processing of karakul pelts as well as most cattle slaughter and processing.

On the other hand, in 1979 out of a GDP of R1,425 million only a little less than R30 million was spread between 250,000 subsistence farmers and their dependents. This meagre income is supplemented by contract wage labour. In all, the income of blacks is only 12% of GDP compared with 24% for whites, the rest going to businesses or the state.

Radical inequality

The stark polarisation of Namibia's economy is partly geographically determined. The territory is extremely well endowed with a limited number of resources and extremely unfavoured in most others. This would lead to a high level of external trade under any political system. However, some aspects of today's polarised pattern are far from inevitable.

Subsidies and controls have been used to discourage diversification of production towards local demand. On the one hand, prices and subsidies favour export goods, such as cattle, rather than goods produced and consumed at home, such as crops. On the other hand, Africans earn so little because of the low-wage contract system, and barriers to successful agriculture are sufficiently great, that they do not spend enough to encourage local producers. Despite the very high ratio of state revenue to GDP — 40% in 1979 compared with 20-25% in most low- to middle-output African states — only the white minority has benefited from consumption subsidies and public services of any quantity or quality.

Though 68% of white children go to secondary school only 3% of African children get past Form One; in Form Two they are likely to be taught in classes of 45-50. At the end of the 1960s life expectancy for Ovambo men was 31 years; for Europeans 65 years. Public services are distributed per capita on a ten to one basis in favour of whites. The apparent exceptions only prove the rule. Veterinary services for African cattle are good, to avert risks of epidemics which could spread to white ranches; road development in the north has been spectacular, as a feeder system to facilitate troop movements for military operations. Under the DTA most of the large state revenues are being used to prop up 'ethnic authorities', administrators, police and 'home guard'. The new free enterprise philosophy emanating from Pretoria means that even whites now will begin to feel economic pressures as subsidies are cut back.

The DTA's strategy of sponsoring the creation of a tiny black middle class, even were it to succeed, would not remove the radical inequalities of Namibia's society. Such a middle class would, of course, be even smaller than the one Pretoria hopes to create in the Republic. The plight of the unemployed and destitute in reserves and rural areas, many fed in the past at mission stations, would remain unchanged unless dramatic wage increases were made to all black workers, and unless a major distribution of land took place.

But the strategy cannot possibly succeed in the 'free enterprise' climate of DTA policy; black private landowners outside the ranks of DTA politicians are virtually non-existent, and cannot come into being without state help. Black businessmen, similarly, may be counted on one hand. In 1977, with the exception of primary school teachers and nurses, 93% of managerial and professional jobs were held by whites; the 7% were on the whole 'Coloureds'. Only 5,000 Africans had received secondary education at that date let alone risen in the civil service from the lower ranks where blacks were beginning to be recruited.*

Stagnation and decline

The DTA has presided over a major stagnation and decline in the Namibian economy. By 1978, overfishing by South African, Soviet and European fishing fleets had almost destroyed one of Namibia's major industries. From 1,500,000 tonnes in 1968 catches dropped to less than 150,000 tonnes. Canning factories now lie idle while canned Chilean fish, processed in machinery exported from Walvis Bay, is now being imported. The South African fleet is now fishing in Chilean waters.

Lack of 'investor confidence' grows and, with the uncertainty over Namibia's future, most mining companies are refusing to move from exploration to the investment of further capital. During 1980-1981, world gluts of high-grade diamonds caused probably 25-30% cut-backs in De Beers' production at Oranjemund. With mining now forming some 52% of GDP, fluctuations in production may be critical. Only cattle sales have risen, though recent lung disease has reduced exports.

---

* In contrast, secondary education organised abroad by SWAPO was by 1981, with over 3,000 students, comparable with the total internal African Forms 2-5 enrolment. Post-secondary training at perhaps 500 was significantly higher.

Namibia is suffering from inflation, rising from 9% in 1978 to perhaps 15% per annum in 1981. The wage increases of the mining sector, and smaller increases in others, do not compensate for rising food prices for the majority of the black population. With the disruption of farming as a result of the war in the north, with drought — a perennial danger —, with growing unemployment and with the flight of large numbers of people to the towns, the plight of Namibia's agricultural majority has worsened sharply.

The basic apartheid political economy, under the impact of changes required for a 'national solution', has produced a widening in the gap between the employed urban residents and the rural majority. A handful of blacks, DTA politicians, government employees, and an appreciable number of 'Coloureds', are in a position to buy luxury items and own cars. But for the majority in the war zone growing impoverishment is felt keenly; cotton workers at a new irrigation scheme in the Okavango have been quick to strike while the spectre of starvation is never far from the door of Ovambo farmers; it is likely to become real as the war progressively prohibits planting and settled agriculture, and the present drought continues.

What the Namibian political economy shows today in stark, skeletal terms is the nature of a system based on theft and inconsistent with all of the principles of economic liberalism. Yet, ironically, it is the principles of Adam Smith and the liberal democracy espoused, and to a substantial extent practised, in western Europe, North America and Australasia, that South Africa and the DTA today claim to represent. Those who claim Namibia as a lesson in the success of capitalist development — unless, of course, they are orthodox Communists committed to violent transitions in political economies — do not seem to grasp fully what they are advocating.

Violence in Namibia

Institutional violence

The political economy of Namibia divides the population into two groups along racial lines, three groups if the marginally higher salaried, better housed, 'Cape Coloured' and Rehoboth sub-groups of the South African defined 'Coloured community' is considered. These divisions, created by the political economy and the gross exploitation of its functioning, have determined that Namibia be ruled by coercion rather than by consent. The fundamental injustice and disorder of such a system, which has turned Namibia into an enclave of super-profits scarcely benefiting its black population, is a form of institutional violence in itself.

The role of the state

This system has required force to sustain it, from the genocide practised on the Herero and Nama people to South Africa's systematic repression of black civil and political rights, enforced removal of populations, and pass laws. To sustain forcibly the exploitation of Namibia's human and natural resources has remained an important function of the Namibian colonial state from its inception. But a second, no less important, function has been to channel this wealth in the interests of its major beneficiaries, represented latterly in its National Assembly, but to a far greater degree in Pretoria and in the board rooms of the transnationals.

The introduction of the apartheid system, channelling and controlling the movement of labour into the export economy, has been the most striking state intervention in the last two decades, and represented an expression of the dominant interests in South Africa's National Party. This system gave rise to a new group of tribal state functionaries dependent on an ethnic and regional division of Namibia. But, though the system is economically essential to white ranchers and useful to other small white employers, it is not critical for large corporations seeking stable skilled workforces.

The second important state intervention, brought on by the changing nature of contract labour, now politically more organised and more dispensable, was the enforced creation of the DTA to combat SWAPO. Again, this represented the interests of the dominant section of the National Party, now a group strongly influenced by business and the military. Its goal was an 'independent' Namibia tied to South Africa, hostile to the front line states and liberation movements, and underwriting the continuation of the political economy of theft in multiracial guise.

Divisions among whites

The forceps delivery of the DTA in the 1978 elections produced a rift in the white community; there were sporadic outbreaks of white terrorism, and an entrenchment of the conservative AKTUR. The differences between DTA and AKTUR may be glimpsed from the interest groups supporting them: for AKTUR, expatriate South African state functionaries and parastatal employees plus Afrikaner shopkeepers, farmers and semi-skilled labour; for DTA, most mining companies and other transnationals plus opportunist members of homelands governments with their clients, the 'Namibian' army, and most German farmers and shopkeepers.

Attitudes to independence vary considerably between the foreign-dominated mining industry ('Let it be') and the Afrikaner-controlled stock-rearing and fishing industries ('Stop it at all costs'). Their positions have elements of economic rationality. The rates of profit per black worker in the mining industry are very high: from R40,000 per man at Rössing to R28,000 at Oranjemund and R5,000 at Tsumeb. However, for farms employing eight men the comparable figure in the stock-rearing industry is R1,500 per man. Since any independent Namibian government would be obliged to raise wages to Poverty Datum Line levels to retain political credibility, this would have dramatically different results in the two industries. While a substantial number of stock-rearers would be put out of business, or have to dip into their own incomes, mining profits would merely be reduced by 5%. Not surprisingly, AKTUR won the second-tier elections on the votes of Afrikaner farmers and South African public service employees, both groups perceiving their livelihoods to be at stake, while the DTA was given sympathetic hearings by right-wing parties in Europe, and by transnationals.

So Namibia's political economy has today divided both blacks from whites, and whites from whites. But if it is an expression of the major financial interests at work in South Africa's National Party, it demonstrates no less the growing importance of South Africa's Defence Forces in Pretoria's counsels of state.

From implicit to open violence

For much of the period of South Africa's occupation of Namibia, overt state violence remained an unspoken threat shoring up unjust legislation and ready to enforce the institutional violence that kept blacks from access to the territory's wealth and deprived them of civil and political rights. An all-white judiciary — there are less than five blacks practising law in Namibia, and only one barrister — tried blacks, and a vigilant white community reported dissidents to the police. Since the shooting of demonstrators in 1959, SWAPO members have been regularly detained and tortured.

Since the independence of Angola, however, the repression of black political aspirations has required more overt and sustained use of violence by the state. To contain the forces of PLAN increasing numbers of South African troops were drawn into Namibia. From 1978 onwards Namibia became a 'military problem' conceived within the total strategy of Pretoria's military planners. The rising pool of unemployed was drawn on for conscripts to join the SADF. State violence had been answered by the violence of a liberation war. This war, no less than the long-term interests of the beneficiaries of Namibia's economy, of whose intrinsic violence it represents an extension, now determines the future of Namibia.

South Africa's Colonial War

The development of the war

Owing to strict military censorship, it is very difficult, particularly for South Africans, to obtain an accurate impression of the war in Namibia and Angola. At present, there are perhaps between 1,000-2,000 PLAN troops at any one time in Namibia, and possibly as many as 5,000 training in Angola. Their tactics have been the conventional guerrilla ones of limited attacks from a politically supportive base amongst the people: sabotage of key communications and some economic targets, mining of roads used by the military, ambush and direct assault on military installations, and the killing of collaborators. In the earliest stages of the war, military activity was limited to the Caprivi and Okavango regions closest to bases in Zambia. A major expansion of the war took place after 1976, when bases began to be established in southern Angola, and a new front opened in Ovamboland. With the exception of the extensive mining of roads, to which South Africa also contributes, PLAN's tactics have been to avoid civilian casualties and to respect mission property and personnel.

South Africa's strategy against PLAN, has passed through three major stages: a slow build-up of troops until after Angolan independence, saturation of the northern regions of Caprivi, Okavango and Ovamboland with major influxes of troops from 1976-1979, and from mid-1980 sustained attacks on Angola, increasingly directed against Angolan infrastructure, civilian and military targets. This last phase of the war has seen a dramatic build-up of South African troops to reach levels estimated by observers at 90,000. Since June 1981 an extremely large South African army has been massed along and inside the Angolan border.

War with Angola

The escalation of the war in Ovamboland since 1978 has been very marked, and from 1979-1981 it has extended to the Kaokoveld in the west, and sporadically to the Tsumeb-Grootfontein-Otavi triangle, and is nearing the Okahandja district north of Windhoek. During this period air and land strikes into Angola have grown in intensity, scope and duration with some irregular units operating permanently inside Angola's borders. In this most recent phase of the war, the use of UNITA insurgents, and mercenary forces (especially ex-Rhodesian and Portuguese paramilitary and irregular units), enabled much of the war in southern Angola, until recently, to be kept hidden from the world press.

Today the Angolan-Namibian border has ceased to exist in all but name and much of southern Angola, Kuando Kubango, Kunene, Mocamedes and Huila provinces are being depopulated as people flee to the towns along the Benguela railway. Streams of refugees pass backwards and forwards across the free-fire zone proclaimed by South Africa at the border, looking for food and shelter, or trading in goats, following the vicissitudes of war. Military spokesmen for South Africa now openly admit that 'special tactics', prolonged periods of operations from bases inside Angola, are being used by South African forces.

The incursion during August-September 1981 of four large motorised columns, and the destruction of the town of Cahama, represented a major new development in the war. Accompanied by repeated air-strikes, South African troops engaged Angolan army units in Xangongo and Ongiva, fighting pitched battles up to 120 miles inside Kunene Province. South African authorities now openly admitted fighting FAPLA (Angolan Security Forces) and the intensity of the incursion brought about widespread international denunciation of the South African occupation of southern Angola. Wide press coverage finally brought home to western readers that the Namibian war had, to all intents and purposes, become a war with Angola, a situation that had prevailed for some two years.

The level of this warfare may be glimpsed from the films of television crews and the reports of other witnesses visiting southern Angola. According to a communiqué issued by the Ministry of Defence in Luanda, for the half-year ending 31 December 1980 400 civilians and 85 Angolan soldiers are estimated to have been killed, and 640 civilians and 97 soldiers injured. The large town of Lubango had been bombed and considerable destruction of railways, bridges, and buildings had taken place.* In a major engagement at Cuamato, South African Puma helicopters supported by ground forces made a direct attack on Angolan troops. Sources in Namibia noted daily waves of South African bombers flying into Angola from Ondangua airforce base for the three weeks following the Geneva Conference in January 1981. The activities of the notorious 32 Buffalo battalion operating into Angola from Rundu have been confirmed by the British mercenary, Trevor Edwards. He made it plain that the battalion, recruited largely from dissident Angolans, had as its principal target Angolan civilians, who were killed indiscriminately during patrols. The same indiscriminate killing of civilians took place in waves of air-strikes in late August in which targets such as the towns of Cahama and Tchibemba, and civilian road traffic, were hit.

These tactics are entirely consistent with South Africa's 'total

---

* Lubango was again extensively bombed in March 1981.

strategy' theories. Direct attacks on the populations of neighbouring states follow logically from attacks on their economic infrastructure, a policy put into practice during the last three years of the Smith regime in Rhodesia. The purpose of such warfare, some observers believe, is not merely to deny SWAPO forces passage into Namibia and to put pressure on the front-line states to deliver SWAPO to the conference table, but also to remind the front-line states of the cost of housing South African liberation movements in the future. In the minds of Pretoria's strategists, it is the future struggle for South Africa which is being fought out in southern Angola rather than control over Namibia.

Caprivi and Okavango
The saturation of the northern region of Namibia by South African forces, and the invasion of south-west Zambia and Angola in early 1980, has made any major PLAN Offensive in Caprivi difficult. In consequence Caprivi has been 'pacified' for the past four years by the SADF. Attempts have been made by South Africa to stimulate the redevelopment of the Caprivi African National Union, both as a way of sowing regional discord in SWAPO's ranks, and to limit support for PLAN in Caprivi, (CANU dissolved in 1964 and joined SWAPO). These attempts resulted in the expulsion of several SWAPO members including the then acting vice-president, Mishake Muyongo, now leading a tiny South African-recognised CANU in Caprivi.

To a lesser extent, the SADF have also been successful in the Okavango region, where they set up a series of 'protected villages' along the Kavango river, and carried out savage reprisal raids in response to PLAN attacks. In consequence, visitors to Namibia are most likely to be given 'facility trips' to Okavango and Caprivi, from where journalists and parliamentarians dutifully report that the SADF have everything under control. This pattern was followed by a publicity trip of the entire South African cabinet to Namibia in June 1981.

Ovamboland
The reality is dramatically different in Ovamboland, where visitors are closely escorted and flown by helicopter to carefully selected army bases. Here, PLAN has made rapid gains since 1976. The celebrated Ruacana Falls Dam power station has been rendered unusable through sabotage of power lines to the south, and a new electricity supply is having to be brought up from South Africa's grid. Telegraph poles and lines are rarely left intact for more than short periods in Ovamboland, and bridges even on main roads are regularly blown up; the bridge over the main north-south Oshakati-Tsumeb road was holed in February 1981. The town of Oshakati had been shelled a month

earlier, probably as a reprisal for the merciless bombing of southern Angola. In 1980 a major strike destroyed planes of the South African airforce at Ondangua.

The success of PLAN's operations in Ovamboland has allowed the area of guerrilla activity to push south, west into Kaokoveld, and east back into Okavango, permitting a major offensive to begin in June 1981. Despite the influx of many more South African troops, from the Geneva Conference until June, and further dramatic increases since, the war is going badly for the occupation forces and SWAPO is barely being contained. A current saying is that after sunset the government of Namibia changes and SWAPO is in uncontested control of Ovamboland.

The impact of PLAN's successful prosecution of its guerrilla strategy in Ovamboland on South African troops has been very great. Morale appears to be low and even the brief three-month tour of duty in the 'operational area' is widely disliked. Temperatures in the hottest months rise to 43°C and patrols in the inhospitable Namibian bush increasingly risk ambush by PLAN forces. Only a small fraction of SADF forces in Namibia seek contact; the shelling of Oshakati, for example, took place at midnight, but only at 10.00 the next morning did a patrol venture out in 'hot pursuit'. Attempts to engage PLAN inside Namibia are limited to special tracker units, composed of cavalry, motor-cycle brigades and bushmen; these call in airborne troops for the 'kill'. Prolonged boredom, interspersed by routine patrols in which conscript troops pray not to meet PLAN, describes much of South Africa's colonial war.

The undermining of the morale of the SADF in an unwinnable war, in what most troops see as a foreign country, is an important factor in military strategists' thinking. Equally important, as shown in Rhodesia, is the sapping of civilian morale as farms are abandoned and whites pack up and leave, especially in the 'triangle of death' around Otavi. The need to keep South African casualties to a minimum, for domestic political reasons, deserters suggest, determines a policy of indiscriminate attacks on black civilians in whose company guerrillas are found. Resistance to the war, growing amongst white students and church groups inside South Africa, has begun to cast Namibia in the role of the Afrikaners' Vietnam.

The logic of this set of circumstances has dictated spectacular raids into Angola, the maximum use of irregular and insurgent Angolan forces, together with mercenaries, in combat. More important it has demanded the Namibianisation of the war. In this way, the impact of the war on South Africa through its conscript army might be minimised. At the same time, Namibia, like Rhodesia before it, could be used as a testing ground for counter-insurgency techniques to be used ultimately against the African National Congress in the growing struggle for South Africa itself.

Namibianisation of the War

Conscription

Two principal schemes have characterised South Africa's attempt to Namibianise the war: recruitment of seven 'ethnic' battalions of 600 soldiers each, and the introduction of conscription for all Namibians aged 16-25. The need to introduce conscription is some measure of the relative failure of the 'ethnic' battalions strategy, but it also indicates Pretoria's need to create the appearance of an 'independent' SWA Defence Force to 'replace' the South African command. But conscription has been no less a resounding failure. In a number of approaches to the Administrator-General, the churches warned of the dire consequences, and appealed for it not to be put into practice. Despite their appeals and international protest, conscription began officially on 1 January 1981.*

Reaction to the threat of conscription was great in both the north and in the Katutura township of Windhoek. It was politically counter-productive; households which had successfully kept out of politics now had to take sides. Their young male members had either to fight their fellow Namibians on behalf of South Africa, or flee to SWAPO across the border. Between December 1980 and March 1981, it is estimated, at least 8,000 young Namibians fled to join SWAPO. From Katutura many went across the Botswana border. So great was the exodus that the SADF attempted to broadcast the message that conscription would not apply in the northern regions which already had 'ethnic' battalions, Kavango, Ovambo and Caprivi. Form Five in one school in Ovamboland — one of the few remaining — tells the story today: 26 girls, 5 boys.

Conscription has involved virtual pressganging and the taking of under-aged boys for training at Walvis Bay and other camps. The conscription of SWAPO members has been followed up in at least one instance. In late April a group of new conscripts were required to identify their political allegiance at Okahandja camp. A group of 28 'Coloured' conscripts admitted to being in favour of SWAPO. They were immediately disarmed and taken to an undisclosed destination in the 'operational area' for an 'orientation programme'. On 12 June 1981, a major demonstration by their parents took place in Windhoek to protest at their treatment and their conscription.

---

* See Appendix B.

The 'omakakunya'

Nonetheless, under the impact of the war, near-starvation and widespread unemployment some 'willing' conscripts have come forward. With influx control lifted, people from the north have flocked to Katutura, where every black home houses relatives, sleeping rough or in kitchens in preference to living in the war zone. Pressure to get paid employment, even in the army, is very great. The home guard, a poorly paid militia that affords opportunities for extortion and pillage, has attracted many near criminals in the north.

The popular generic name for Namibians fighting for South Africa is *omakakunya* (contemptible little creatures who gnaw the people down to the bone — to eat meat down to the bone is an act of extreme shame for Ovambos). It expresses well how people feel about them. They are renowned for heavy drinking, occasional rape, and beating up of civilians, particularly well educated people like schoolteachers against whom they harbour particular grudges and suspicions. Unaccustomed to handling arms, and sometimes simpleminded, they are a serious danger to life and property. Like the Muzorewa and Sithole auxiliaries in Zimbabwe in 1978-1980, their hold over daily life in Ovamboland has consolidated the already considerable local support for SWAPO's better disciplined forces. The loyalty of the *omakakunya* and of many minor DTA officials and their clients is questionable; in many cases they will terminate their relationships when they cease to be profitable. The oft-repeated phrase of local observers is that the DTA is 'glued together with money'.

The cancer in society

Apart from the South African soldiers, *omakakunya* and the *amati* ('friends', the popular name for PLAN), Namibians are also growing accustomed to the 'dirty tricks' department of the South African Defence Forces. Trained at military bases inside South Africa, special *koevoet* squads with commando skills operate both in Angola and Namibia, killing SWAPO members, posing as guerrillas and abducting individuals for interrogation by torture. These units may have been strengthened by experienced ex-Selous scouts since Zimbabwe's independence. The blowing up of the Evangelical Lutheran OvamboKavango Church Press at Oniipa in November 1980 and St. Mary's Anglican seminary at Odibo in June 1981 illustrate operations against the churches. Government *mujibas* (special constables) are being used to spy on villagers and to report guerrilla movements, another technique learnt from the guerrilla war in Rhodesia.

The conduct of the war by regular South African troops is hardly less disturbing. Suspicion that PLAN has visited a village may have a variety of consequences: huts burnt down, an indiscriminate air-strike, hand-grenades thrown into kraals, or, more typically, beatings and electric shock torture of villagers to elicit information. Police and military torture of detainees in the numerous detention centres dotted around the country, or in unmarked houses in urban areas, has continued unabated under the DTA despite protests from church leaders. Its extent in 1978 was fully documented in a publication by the then Superior-Provincial of the Oblate Fathers in Namibia, Heinz Hunke, and by the secretary of the Christian Centre, Justin Ellis, *Torture: A Cancer in our Society* (republished by CIIR/BCC 1978). Evidence from a number of different sources indicates that torture continues to be used systematically by police and army in Namibia today.

As in Zimbabwe's guerrilla war, little attempt is made by government forces to distinguish between civilians and guerrillas; the telling assumption seems to be made that everyone supports 'the enemy', an assumption that has resulted in massacres of large groups of people during the past year alone.* The steady killing of curfew-breakers, often children on harmless errands, passes almost without comment. The high casualty figures issued by the SADF for SWAPO 'kills' highlight the penalties for this widespread support for PLAN; perhaps more than 60% of these 'kills' are civilians caught in cross-fire, found in a village harbouring PLAN, accidentally killed, or deliberately murdered in reprisal.

The agony of Ovamboland

The suffering of the people in Ovamboland, as all church leaders stress with growing anguish, is now immense. Their daily life is a struggle to escape from paralysing fear. Their land is an armed camp with sandbagged installations for the occupation forces dotted throughout it. Seven secondary schools have shut down in the past two years. Towns like Oshakati are fortresses consisting almost entirely of state functionaries and military personnel, with air-raid shelters and anti-aircraft emplacements, barbed wire and towers reminiscent of the Berlin wall. The massive Ondangua airbase spreads over acres of countryside, a stark reminder of South Africa's immensely superior military technology.

The representatives of the DTA live behind wire fences and high sandbagged walls, protected from the people that they claim to represent. The ex-chairman of the executive committee of the Ovambo homeland administration, Pastor Ndjoba, lives in a large house sand-bagged to the eaves; over ten members of the Ovambo Legislative Assembly have been assassinated in the past two years. Armoured per-

* See Appendix A.

sonnel carriers and heavily armoured vehicles ferry troops and state functionaries from one enclave to another over roads swept daily for mines. Large dumps of vehicles outside military camps, wrecked by mines, provide mute evidence of how effective mine-laying has become. Troops of the occupation forces travel strapped into bullet-proof metal containers, only the tips of their rifles and mulberry-shaped grenades visible. The terrible logic of apartheid violence, a burgeoning militarism, finds its fullest expression in the dust and military hardware of Ovamboland in late 1981.

3 A Future for Namibia

After Geneva, January 1981

Stalling tactics

South Africa's style of negotiating, viz. military action and building stumbling blocks to complicate and delay agreement, continued throughout 1980. The implementation of Resolution 435, which formed the basis for negotiations, was consistently debated in the abstract, South Africa refusing to admit any time-scale for future action. Both Pretoria and the DTA persistently complained about the lack of impartiality of the United Nations. Despite the illegality of the South African occupation and their fraudulent 1978 elections, demand for the UN General Assembly to repudiate its 1967 recognition of SWAPO as the sole and authentic representative of the Namibian people became a sticking point.

Somewhat illogically, the United Nations softpedalled the obvious reply. South Africa, illegally in Namibia and a directly interested party, could not conceivably be characterised as 'impartial'. Yet her demands meant that she would be responsible for the handling of the actual civil and electoral machinery during transition. For South Africa to dwell on impartiality was, therefore, at the best a disingenuous attempt to disguise reality, at worst more stalling tactics.

The conference

South Africa agreed to a pre-implementation conference in Geneva, it seems likely, in the hope of giving the DTA a certain legitimacy as a negotiating partner. Essential to this propaganda exercise was that the DTA should take its place opposite SWAPO at the negotiating table. A perhaps acceptable setting would have been a Lancaster House style conference in which a third party — attempts were made to lure the front line states — hammered out a settlement between the DTA and SWAPO. This would have permitted South Africa to withdraw gracefully with the blame for a future SWAPO government resting on the 'miscalculation' and 'incompetence' of Mr Mudge and the Administrator-General, Mr Hough. It would have had the added bonus of introducing a range of constitutional constraints on SWAPO limiting the possibilities of transforming Namibia's economy.

For years the United Nations had inched forward on the basis of Resolution 435. To jettison these gains at this point on the high seas of a Lancaster House would have been irresponsible folly. The comparable power to Britain in Rhodesia was the UN Council for Namibia, studiously ignored by South Africa, and unadapted to diplomatic brinkmanship even had Pretoria accepted it. For SWAPO to have accepted as an equal the crumbling DTA alliance, a body that had convincingly been shown to represent only the aspirations of South Africa's clients, would have been equally foolish. In the event, a compromise formula was devised whereby the South African delegation 'contained' the DTA, AKTUR and some other politically insignificant groupings. The delegates assembled in Geneva on 5 January 1981 at the invitation of the United Nations.

As a propaganda exercise for the DTA, Geneva proved a resounding flop. The DTA delegates combined the hysteria of drowning men with an amalgam of invective and threats quite uncongenial to the world's press. A carefully prepared speech by Mr Mudge, dwelling on 'trust and confidence', qualities associated with a two-year breathing space for the DTA, could do little to reverse the impression that their lack of faith in the UN was equalled only by their lack of faith in themselves and the South Africans. Press coverage of SWAPO, on the other hand, reflected their cautious diplomacy and substantive plans for the future; following an earlier trend in the South African English-language press, SWAPO were presented as a potential future government of Namibia.*

Despite SWAPO's restraint and its willingness to sign an immediate ceasefire and abide by Resolution 435, even including a readiness to lose the unique recognition of the UN during transition,

---

* This probably indicated some coming to terms with the inevitability of a future SWAPO government by the transnationals like Anglo-American, a process which had already begun by 1980. In contrast reactions to the DTA black leaders were hostile. Their strident assertions that if 'unleashed' they could end the war in six weeks called forth laughter from the press; their plea for two years of peace so that SWAPO would not win the election as the party that brought peace struck nobody — including South Africa — as realistic and amounted to an open admission that they would lose a 1981 election. Indeed Mr Mudge at one point admitted that in a 1981 election the results would parallel those of the Zimbabwean elections of the previous year.

South Africa was unwilling to sign even a Declaration of Intent. 'Trust and confidence' in the UN were allegedly lacking. Elections, which in 1978 South Africa had insisted on rushing through without UN supervision, had in 1981 become 'premature' — with UN supervision.

South Africa's motives

That South Africa wrecked the Geneva Conference within the allotted week surprised few. That it did so without providing the Contact Group and the United Nations with even the meanest scrap to take home as 'a sign of forward movement', and all the hallowed excuses for voting against UN sanctions, surprised many.

This indifference to diplomatic niceties was attributable to four main factors: the two usually stressed are Mr P.W. Botha's need to strengthen his position through a general election, and the conjunction of a Conservative government in Britain with the strong possibility of a new Africa policy emerging from the Reagan administration in the USA. A UK/USA conservative alliance spelt a possible new malleability in the Contact Group.

Possibly equally important, and complementary, were the increasing lack of coherence in the Contact Group and South Africa's lack of any clear idea how to disengage from Namibia, at this point, without a landslide victory for SWAPO in UN elections. By the end of the Geneva talks, it was clear that West Germany and France, (even before the Mitterrand government came to power) had hardened their stand for Resolution 435 and the implementation of the proposals as they stood. The German foreign minister, in particular, was relatively unwilling to antagonise SWAPO by negotiating further concessions to South Africa, and found support from Canada and France. Given the USA's swing in the opposite direction, South Africa could reasonably count on the Contact Group being unable to sustain a united initiative to its conclusion.

The Reagan administration

The first indication of the new administration's southern Africa policy, in as much as the dissonant emphases and personality clashes amounted to a credible unified strategy, was pleasing to South Africa and confirmed their high expectations. The National Security State ideology fostered by Mr P.W. Botha and his total strategy theorists found echoes in Washington. In the new line 'American interests' were to be equated with strategic minerals and a struggle against 'Soviet expansionism' and 'international terrorism' rather than with flabby commitments to human rights. In its more sophisticated formulations, this policy found a place for 'modernising autocracies', a term applicable to a future South Africa ruled by its National Security Council with the military pushing through 'reforms' and parliament 'in abeyance'.

While President Reagan would ritually continue to deplore apartheid, he would also place South Africa more firmly in the western camp by drawing on a common Manichean faith that Africa was the coming battleground between 'communism' and 'the west'. The South African foreign minister was tellingly preceded to Washington by the head of South African military intelligence, Lt General P.W. van Westerhuizen, and a four-man military mission.* The central issue at stake in Namibia had become whether South Africa would fight 'communism' on the Angola-Namibia border or at the Orange River. The fate of Namibia, as indeed that of all South Africa, was slipping into military hands.

For the USA, this military decision was properly linked to a regional perspective in which support for UNITA and the removal of 20,000 Cuban troops from Angola was a top priority. As South Africa had calculated, the powerful right wing of the Reagan administration saw the USA's commitment to Resolution 435 as nominal and subordinate to the greater good of stopping Soviet 'expansion'. The approach was singularly simple minded. Angola, both informally and in an address by its foreign minister to a US business dinner, has clearly indicated that given freedom from South African military incursions it would rapidly phase out foreign combat troops. This perception is shared by US banks, transnationals and, above all, Gulf Oil. They see Angola as a pragmatic and dependable partner and have pressed both the Carter and Reagan administration to establish normal diplomatic relations with it.

By May 1981, under American pressure, the Contact Group was in disarray with public statements manifestly papering over cracks between the USA, UK and other members, much to Pretoria's delight. The formula reached was that 'improvements' would be made to Resolution 435: property rights would be guaranteed together with a multi-party system with constitutional safeguards for the whites, whilst the independence government would be 'neutral'. The Americans had hoped to peddle around southern Africa, in a burst of shuttle diplomacy, a constitution drawn up by the team of ill-defined 'experts'. One month later, with France's foreign minister Cheysson and the front line states drawing a firm line under Washington's flirtation with Pretoria, the Namibia issue temporarily dropped below

---

* Once their presence became known to the Press, they were asked to leave.

the horizon of US foreign policy. In Windhoek, the National Assembly was pressing successfully for the role of AG to be reduced to that of Governor-General and UNTAG's presence in Namibia during any transition was now, for them, unacceptable. There was no effective pressure being exerted on South Africa save by SWAPO, no apparent end to the suffering of Namibians in the war zone, and no immediate possibility of a new conference to bring Namibia to independence and a peaceful future.

Towards a future for Namibia

SWAPO's political organisation and policy-making
In the judgement of most observers, the majority of Namibians would vote for SWAPO in free and fair elections. Any peaceful solution to the conflict in Namibia that allows the democratic will of this majority to be expressed would give rise to a SWAPO government. It therefore seems important to present what SWAPO envisages as the future for Namibia, policies that are often lost from sight in the rhetoric of the propaganda war being fought over the future of the territory.

During the second half of the 1970s, SWAPO was steadily developing, refining and articulating its position. Only one part of the strategy related to PLAN and the steadily growing guerrilla war, strategically not dissimilar to ZANLA's campaign in Zimbawe. A second related to diplomacy and the mobilisation of international opinion to isolate South Africa and to win verbal, political and material support for SWAPO.

Political organisation inside Namibia continued with attempts to reactivate the National Union of Namibian Workers in 1977, and its wide circulation of a policy manifesto in several languages during the next year. SWAPO became increasingly involved in grassroots worker organisations and in the strikes of 1978-1981. Finally, and perhaps least widely known, has been the articulation of a political economy for an independent Namibia, and the beginnings of manpower development and pre-planning towards its implementation.

The current widespread support for SWAPO at home and internationally is the product of these efforts stemming from two decades of organisation. Inside Namibia the same two decades have seen repeated arrests, torture, and detention of internal SWAPO members and leaders with a growing probability that the movement will be banned finally under the DTA. The building of SWAPO's base in the territory has produced lives of outstanding courage and fortitude: men like Axel Johannes, now aged 36, who has spent one third of his life intermittently in prison and in detention, suffering beating and torture, before finally fleeing the country.

Problems of building a movement

The year 1976 was a turning point for SWAPO; after attempting to form broad popular fronts with other parties, SWAPO finally withdrew from the Namibia National Convention, taking with it large numbers of supporters amongst Nama-speaking and Herero-speaking political groups, along with a faction of the 'Basters' (descendents of Europeans and Nama) of Rebohoth. With the SWAPO Youth League recruiting during the school boycotts, this influx of supporters firmly established SWAPO's position as a national party. The post-1976 non-SWAPO politicians who were left were a rather unpromising ragbag with the notable exception of Chief Clemens Kapuuo; as the successor to the famous nationalist chief Kutako, he initially possessed some political capital. The other homelands leaders were mostly wedded to South African concepts of ethnicity and the power and pay cheques that went with them.

A central internal problem for SWAPO was the difficulty of maintaining a disciplined movement in the face of infiltration by South African agents. A secondary problem was co-ordination between SWAPO's external headquarters in Luanda and the internal party in Windhoek. South Africa's decision not to ban SWAPO outright may have been associated with hopes of creating a rift between 'internal' and 'external' wings, or, probably, with fear of local and international reaction. The dismissal of the deputy National Chairman, Daniel Tjongarero, after prolonged police interrogation in Windhoek during January 1979, illustrates one advantage for South Africa of allowing nominal 'legality' for SWAPO: at periodic intervals high SWAPO officials could be detained and then released, sowing doubts about their future loyalty to the party.

A more extensive break occurred when SWAPO's secretary for information and publicity, Mr Andreas Shipanga, began to dispute the party leadership with the president, Sam Nujoma, during 1976. Along with Herman Toivo Ya Toivo, still serving a sentence on Robben Island (44 other SWAPO members are also detained in the Republic), he was a founder member of the Ovambo Peoples' Organisation (OPO) in Cape Town. He was detained by SWAPO for two years, mostly in Tanzania, with some 200 followers who were finally screened, rejoined SWAPO or went to a United Nations refugee camp. Shipanga himself and a few others returned to Namibia to form the SWAPO (Democrats).* The South African government

---

* While occasionally flirting with South African attempts to create new coalitions, Shipanga has maintained a verbally anti-South African stance combined with a great bitterness towards SWAPO, as well as towards the Ovambo homeland authorities. Reports suggest that the South African government also offered Hermann Toivo Ya Toivo his freedom if he joined Shipanga; he remains in prison.

used these detentions to great effect, calling for the release of 'SWAPO detainees' long after they had all been freed, exploiting the issue to cast doubt on the United Nations' impartiality.

Attempts to turn SWAPO(D) and CANU into serious opposition parties for electoral purposes are undoubtedly destined to fail whatever coalitions are proposed. The highest estimates give Shipanga 5% of the vote while CANU would be lucky to poll more than 300 votes in a free election. In contrast, the SWAPO Youth League are able to gather crowds of 3,000-4,000 in Katutura to protest against conscription, and visitors to Katutura near the 'Ovambo Hostel' are greeted with SWAPO salutes.

The frequently painted picture that SWAPO is the party of the gun is belied by their consistent willingness to agree to a ceasefire, provided it is followed reasonably promptly by UN-supervised elections. PLAN engages in political education as well as warfare, with meetings taking place openly during the day in the north as guerrillas mingle freely with the local population. Not only have SWAPO made considerable concessions to get to the polling booth, agreeing to 15 South African bases in the DMZ and waiving their UN status during transition, but they have, unlike the DTA, a substantive programme for a future Namibia in the interests of the majority of its people.

SWAPO's programme

SWAPO's first detailed set of political economic goals were contained in its 1976 *Programme of Action*. On the basis of these it has produced the main elements of manpower development, an agricultural sector reform, a language policy, and an educational and health strategy. Despite the difficulty of data collection and the contradictory demands of the war and their wide-ranging diplomatic offensive, SWAPO has built up a set of goals, with the technical and material means to achieve them, considerably in advance of any other African pre-independence movement.

When feasible these policies have been put into practice. Education, health, agriculture and public administration methods are implemented in the numerous refugee centres. Manpower programmes now number up to 4,000, with students working from artisanal to second university degree levels. The UN Institute for Namibia is the best known and one of the key units in this programme, but now numbers less than 10% of the total students involved in other programmes. Similarly SWAPO is participating in the UN 'Nationhood Programme' and has gained membership in most UN agencies through the UN Council for Namibia. The ability of SWAPO to obtain finance for this wide range of research and training projects, now costing perhaps R20 million, excluding direct support for refugees, is an index of the priority it places on non-military preparations for independence, as well as the strong international commitment to this aspect of SWAPO's activity.

The SWAPO programme for a future independent Namibia is pragmatic and coherent given the deformities of the colonial economy. SWAPO indicated during the Geneva Conference that the Rössing mine would be kept open, and the sale of its uranium oxide to European nuclear power plants would be continued according to economic, not political, criteria. This would imply, implicitly, the retention of an external management, though not necessarily that of RTZ. Similarly, the expulsion and sacking of competent white farmers, civil servants and technical personnel was excluded during the transition period after independence, nor was the confiscation of small businesses envisaged. Their objections to the Rössing mine seem to be that its establishment by RTZ after 1966 was illegal and, they believe, the conditions of its workers inadequate and, probably, unsafe. It objects to whites as exploitative employers, rather than, as may be necessary in the short term, a temporarily well-paid elite. Following the experience of Zimbabwe, rather than that of Mozambique, it appears that every attempt will be made to limit the precipitate flight of skilled personnel needed to avoid a breakdown in the country's complex industries.

General economic strategy

The *Programme of Action* foresees a post-independence transition period with mixed state, co-operative, private and joint ownership of the country's productive forces. If Zimbabwe becomes the model, such a period prior to a movement to socialism, described as 'bringing all major means of production and exchange into the ownership of the people', may be prolonged. Partial public ownership of key sectors of the economy, mining, fishing, ranching, banking and finance, and land, seems likely. Titles to non-productive assets, such as homes and savings accounts, and basic property rights of this kind, appear to be assured in this programme. The basic title to productive assets like fish, minerals and land will be regarded as the property of the nation, though not necessarily excluding private occupancy, use and development. South African state corporations seem to be subject to nationalisation without compensation.

Overall economic strategy has as a goal comprehensive agrarian reform in the interests of food security and rural development. Meat and fish industries, for example, would be partially diverted from export to internal consumption, and new processing industries sponsored. The central theme of the SWAPO programme, self-reliance, is highlighted in the promise to sever all links with the Republic of South Africa. Trades unions and co-operatives would be encouraged within the framework of the wider goals of stimulating the greatest possible participation in the country's social, political and economic life. A major effort to provide basic education and vocational training for young people would be carried over from the refugee camps, as would techniques of preventive medicine and rural health care.

Mining is seen as a key source of foreign exchange and surplus for the public sector to finance services and investment in rural development. SWAPO intends to keep all major mines running using a combination of management contracts and joint ventures to preserve technical efficiency and the generation of surplus over an indefinite, but moderately extended period. The diamond industry in Botswana and Tanzania provides an implicit model. SWAPO has quite specifically stated that post-independence involvement by transnationals is acceptable, subject to its being on agreed terms which safeguard Namibian foreign exchange, profitability, employment, training and overall economic control.

But, like all official political programmes, that of SWAPO sometimes indicates wide political preferences rather than precise guidelines for action. There can be no doubt that SWAPO is committed to a socialist path of development. Nonetheless, the experience of Zimbabwe, one of a negotiated transfer of power, has demonstrated that 'scientific socialism', under the harsh constraints of the world economy and South Africa's economic control over the region, is a slow process and a long-term goal. It would be quite impossible for Namibia to disengage overnight from South Africa without ruin. But unlike Zimbabwe or Botswana it has few links that could not be ultimately broken in favour of other external sources or by self-reliance built up over a post-independence decade.

What is certain is that SWAPO's economic strategy will move Namibia towards greater national economic integration and into the common struggle of the independent African states of the region for a co-ordinated effort towards economic liberation through the Southern African Development Co-ordination Conference. In concrete terms this implies the construction of a trans-Kalahari railway to Botswana and Zimbabwe, a major road from Katima Mulilo to Zambia, and the development of highways to Angola.* Joint water use and river agreements between Namibia, Angola and Botswana would also be needed. The retention of Walvis Bay will be important for Namibia.

---

* It may also involve a northern extension of the Namibian rail system from Grootfontein to Ondangua to link up with the proposed north-south interior rail-link in Angola.

However, the re-opening of Swakopmund and the building of alternative port facilities further north would make its continued occupation by South Africa amount to a tedious and expensive diversion of resources rather than being an economic disaster.

The Economic Transformation of Namibia

The problems

The ecological and technological constraints on SWAPO's ability to transform the Namibian economy are great: the deserts and savannah are harsh environments, and the major industries are technically complex, a crucial short- and medium-term limitation given the small number of technically trained Namibians. Namibia is no land flowing with milk and honey in which trial and error is permitted without grave penalties; at least 15,000 expatriate professional and technical personnel will be required during post-independence transition, and many of them are likely to be South African. South African and transnational control over the economy today amounts to a stranglehold. To what extent this level of foreign participation in Namibia's economy is compatible with internal security, and the doubtless radical demands of PLAN's leadership, remains to be seen.

It seems likely that an orderly transfer of personnel and sharing of surplus will be possible in transnationally controlled industry which will readily perceive the alternatives, a loss of access to the country's mineral wealth or a great drop in operating surplus. The clash is most likely to occur in ranching, where either a total commitment to stay or leave, will entail intractable problems of different kinds.

Namibian nationalism, having grown out of the colonial theft of land and control of contract labour, will in the post-independence period be likely to create high expectations that land will be redistributed, wages raised appreciably, and families united. The re-uniting of families with contract labourers in towns and around their workplaces will remove some of the pressure on overcrowded rural areas to which Africans are now effectively confined.

However, without other changes, this would permit only a marginal increase in income for those remaining. The actual operation of resettlement is made much more complex because, at present, most households have one or more members alternating between the 'labour reserve home' and the 'European economy compound'. A settled largely urban labour force would, by eliminating this circular flow, reduce the total number of households with some wage income more rapidly than northern agricultural income per household could possibly be raised.

Some 70,000 refugees already need to be resettled and aided, a number likely to reach 90,000 if SWAPO is banned and the outflow due to conscription continues. Careful planning to avoid bottlenecks in the minute housing construction industry will be needed; estimates suggest that some 100,000-150,000 new dwellings will be required as families are united. Training in building skills will be at a premium.

The raising of wages on low-profit white farms which have benefited from generations of state aid and protection will be another potential area of conflict. At the most, in the absence of increased subsidies to ranching, it will be possible to double wages on ranches and farms over a period of five years, some conservative economists suggest, and this very slow improvement would probably generate rural discontent. Difficulties in dispossessing white farmers of land for redistribution, if a white exodus is to be avoided, will make demands for more good land difficult to satisfy. These demands are likely to be intensified by claims for traditional pre-colonial land subsequently lost after white conquest. This situation will constitute a severe test for the party at local level, which will have to retain mass support and mobilise popular energies without stifling disappointment and discontent.

Resources and allies

The possibilities for Namibia's economic transformation are not, though, as bleak as these substantial problems would suggest. The possibilities for the redistribution of wealth and land are enhanced by the small size of Namibia's population. The removal of South African-sponsored UNITA raids on southern Angola, likely to follow from Namibian independence, will greatly strengthen the Angolan government and its potentially prosperous oil economy. Namibia, linked perhaps by road and rail to a strong and stable Angola, will have a large market for its industrial products in the future.

Post-independence transition will undoubtedly be as critical for Namibia as it has been for Zimbabwe. Non-governmental organisations, and particularly the churches, should even now be investigating the best forms of co-operation with the new government, in the area of assistance to refugees, rehabilitation of war-wounded, care of war orphans and adult literacy. Much work in these fields is already being done based on a growing relationship of mutual trust. The use of church property, particularly the infrastructure of missions belonging to the different denominations in Ovamboland, will certainly be helpful to government during this crisis period. Similarly, the mobilisation of the churches' human resources to assist in rural development, education and community development will be a priority requiring careful discussion and planning.

The Christian churches and the struggle for Namibia 1978-1981

The Council of Churches in Namibia grew out of the ecumenical collaboration of the Windhoek Christian Centre in October 1978 and incorporated all the main denominations except the white Dutch Reformed tradition. Despite the vice-presidency of the council initially being in the hands of the conservative German Lutheran Church (DELK), it was able to express the central concern for social justice of the black Lutheran and Anglican communions. The central problem of the council, however, was to sustain any united voice when this concern was translated into concrete positions in relation to United Nations' proposals and areas readily branded as 'political' by those in the pietistic tradition.

A shift in attitudes

While the council was able to obtain virtual unanimity on issues such as their rejection of the 1978 elections — only DELK refused to sign a joint pastoral letter — issues such as SWAPO bases in Namibia during transition split them on largely racial lines. Strong voices in the churches were silenced by deportation, Winter, Wood, Ellis, Hunke, Klein-Hitpas and dozens of Finnish missionaries in Ovamboland whom the South African's repeatedly accused of being subversive and SWAPO supporters. But the leaven of such men and women had begun to transform white missionary opinion. The Roman Catholic Church, once ultra-cautious and equivocal in its stance, slowly put its weight behind the black Lutheran and Anglican churches, and has finally moved from observer status to full membership of the Council. While lay people in the churches remained split along racial lines, amongst the missionary clergy (over 80% of the Roman Catholic clergy) many have increasingly come to support the nationalist church leaders, Bishops Dumeni (ELOC) and Kauluma (Anglican).

During 1980, with the return of Pastor Dr Albertus Maasdorp to become general-secretary of the Council,* the Namibian Council of Churches increasingly began to participate in the shaping of international opinion over Namibia. Where once it had met with the Contact Group and South African Administrator-General irregularly and only in response to contingencies, it was now becoming an important and active voice initiating international contacts. Bishops Dumeni and Kauluma, as well as the Roman Catholic Bishop of Windhoek, Koppman, and his vicar-general Father Henning, went to Geneva in January 1981 to hold discussions behind the scenes at the Conference.

---

* Pastor Maasdorp had been associate secretary of the Lutheran World Federation in Geneva and had studied in the USA. He had left Namibia in 1973.

Pastor Maasdorp was in Europe six months later to alert the European churches to the dangers of the stalemate in Namibia and the deteriorating conditions in the north.

The appointment of Bishop Boniface Haushiku to take Bishop Koppman's place as the Roman Catholic Bishop of Windhoek inaugurated a new period in which the four key denominations were led by black Namibian churchmen. In a statement to the visiting US delegation to Namibia on 12 June 1981, a new edge had come into the protest of the Council of Churches, a reflection of the more united front of the key churches under the elder statesmanship of Bishop Cleophas Dumeni of ELOC.* While church statements expressed general demands for human rights and spoke of the agony and suffering of people in the northern war zones, scrupulously avoiding any charge of political involvement, there could be no doubt that the Christian churches signing them were at one with the Namibian people in their nationalist aspirations.

The position of the Namibian Council of Churches, representing the body of Christian opinion in Namibia today, is clear on the future of the territory. Initiatives are required from the Contact Group to bring about a speedy implementation of an unchanged Resolution 435. On the tenth anniversary of their open letter to Mr B.J. Vorster in 1971, the leaders of the ELOC and ELC communions wrote to the Prime Minister of South Africa: 'Despite numerous decisions and resolutions by the United Nations and South Africa and despite the cry that the people of Namibia should determine their own future, ten long years have passed without giving them the opportunity to make this decision themselves.'** The immense suffering of the people of northern Namibia, as the statements of the Council make plain, is now a product of South Africa's attempt to play for time and of the vain hope that the DTA may at some distant date become acceptable to the Namibian people.

---

* See Appendix E.
** See Appendix F.

4 Conclusion

The war in Namibia is costing South Africa somewhere near R600 million per annum and the possibility of closer relationships with the United States. The territory has for the first time become a net liability to the Republic; in August 1981 the South African defence budget was increased by a further 30% largely as a result of the Namibian war, and an invasion of Angola's Kunene Province brought down universal condemnation. The cost of shoring up the 'representative' authorities in Namibia's 1981 budget is R208 million, plus a R210 m. loan from South Africa. In April 1981, yet again, three major western powers suffered the embarrassment of voting against United Nations resolutions imposing sanctions on South Africa in the Security Council.

The debate within South Africa

A significant number of Pretoria's military strategists would prefer to fight 'communism' in the desert, on the Orange River frontier backed by the Alexander Bay-Upington string of white settlements, rather than along the relatively porous Kunene-Ovambo-Zambesi line amongst the hostile population of northern Namibia. They point to the increased level of strikes, demonstrations, riots and sabotage in the Republic requiring disengagement of the forces now in Namibia to retain control at home. South Africa has good reason to come to the negotiating table sooner rather than later, with a serious intention of implementing the most favourable version of the UN proposals that bargaining can obtain.

South Africa's underlying position has grown increasingly vulnerable, a trend realised by at least some members of the government and a higher proportion of the Afrikaner military and business elite. The war in Namibia is palpably unwinnable, though some of Pretoria's strategists pretend otherwise, and incursions into Angola, short of setting up a puppet regime in Lubango or Huambo, diplomatically costly and militarily ineffective. International pressure on South Africa over Namibia, however low-key and ineffectual it may seem, is very much stronger than the pressure over the Republic itself and its apartheid system; withdrawal would buy time for apartheid at home. The DTA, on its own admission, would need two years before it could win an election, while the Republic's own intelligence reports, it is said, indicate that time is not on its side; the alliance shows signs of falling apart and support for it declines daily.

On the other hand, withdrawal from Namibia would remove the 'justification' for attacks on Angola as well as making them logistically very difficult. It would radically alter the constraints on Botswana and remove South African troops from Zambia's border along the Caprivi strip. Both these factors would be nails in the coffin of Pretoria's 'constellation' plans and could stimulate the movement for economic independence of the Southern African Development Coordination Conference. The impact on white and black morale in the Republic, evidently with equal and opposite results, might be appreciable at a time of widespread unrest. Finally, South Africa's leadership may have successfully brainwashed itself with its own lurid propaganda image of SWAPO as a bloodthirsty, Soviet front organisation bringing 'Moscow's flag to Walvis Bay', and with the corollary that incursions across the Orange River frontier will play more than a marginal role in the South African liberation struggle.

International reaction

The response to South Africa's 1978-1981 tactics has been fairly uniformly negative even if far from uniformly effective. Even the Reagan administration appears to find South Africa both obdurate in the face of attempts to help it, and so extreme in the formulation and presentation of its positions as to make collaboration with it potentially damaging. The front-line states and the OAU have begun to harden their position. They now reject further negotiations on how to change, rather than how to implement Resolution 435, and have pushed sanctions to a semi-binding two-thirds majority vote at the General Assembly.

The result has been a growing international isolation of South Africa with now only two Security Council members, the UK and the USA, certain to exercise their veto against sanctions. France, now lost to South Africa under the Mitterand administration, may be expected to join with West Germany in, for Pretoria, 'very unhelpful' attitudes to Mr Botha. The blustering verbal confidence of South Africa's leaders, interspersed with bouts of anger, and their febrile grasping after a US alliance that will prove quite unobtainable, beyond covert support, disguise a growing realisation that the diplomatic offensive against the Republic is growing in extent and intensity.

In this slow shift in international opinion, the work of voluntary bodies, many church-related, has been and remains significant. The position of the Scandinavian governments against apartheid and in favour of liberation is built on thirty years of efforts by voluntary groups. Finland's special concern for Namibia flows initially from its missionaries' service to Namibians. The growing pressure on the government of the Netherlands to stop oil supplies to South Africa stems in large part from Christian activist groups, and Royal Dutch Shell clearly fears that it will ultimately be successful. In the USA, church groups have spearheaded education and action campaigns which have made several banks decide that further lending to South Africa was imprudent, and led several state legislatures to pass bills against lending to or investment in the Republic.

The struggle for Namibia is by no means won but South Africa, despite its bold front, knows that it is slowly losing and desperately tries to conceal the reality behind bluster and militarism. Its massive propaganda efforts are designed, above all, to give the impression of power and responsibility, to discourage its opponents and cause them, voluntary bodies and churches alike, to believe that their struggle is hopeless and unworthy of sustained efforts.

Problems of the future

But even assuming that UN-supervised elections take place in the near future, immense problems will face the future government. The historical, ecological, technological, and geopolitical constraints — particularly the lack of trained personnel — facing a new Namibia make those on Zimbabwe seem relatively minor. The possibility of transforming Namibia's economy in the interests of the majority of its people is already limited. SWAPO will not wish to issue unlimited guarantees of property rights, disproportionate political representation for whites, nor saddle the new administration with more constraints than already exist.

SWAPO sees it as particularly illogical to elect a constitutional assembly *after* writing the bulk of the constitution, and undesirable to have an externally drafted constitution as opposed to one formulated by elected representatives. Furthermore, it sees no reason to confer rights over property claims which the International Court of Justice has held invalid. But, if South Africa continues to negotiate, as it has done in the past, with the principal intention of stalling for time, it will be easier next time to cast SWAPO in the role of 'conference wrecker', however unjustly.

'Guarantees' and talk of Lancaster House have a deceptive sweet reasonableness about them. But comparisons with Zimbabwe are especially galling to Namibians. The main military forces in Namibia are not 'domestic' troops made up of white settlers fighting with mercenaries, as emerged in Rhodesia, but a foreign occupation army and airforce from the Republic, only recently augmented by a SWA Defence Force and Police. The United Nations is the legal, if ineffectual, sovereign authority. The parallels to Britain's Lord Carrington and Lord Soames are the UN Council for Namibia's Chairman and the UN Commissioner for Namibia.

South Africa's goals

South Africa sees its dominant interest in Namibia as its own survival, not that of the territory's settler community, as many of them, with growing anxiety, are beginning to realise. Its major geopolitical plan is a 'total strategy' with military and economic components. This is why the fate of southern Angola looms almost as large as that of Namibia in negotiations, and why Pretoria could make the apparently ridiculous suggestion that UNITA should participate in future discussions. The destabilisation of southern Angola has two aims: with the Benguela railway intermittently shut, Zambian copper passes through South Africa and a star in the 'constellation' is held in orbit; Angola remains a key base for *Umkhonto we Sizwe*, the military wing of the ANC, and raids raise the cost of their presence.

There are doubtless differences of opinion in South Africa's leadership over future strategy towards Namibia; certain military leaders, for example, wish to pursue policies of destabilisation and victory over SWAPO as articles of faith. But the degree to which these differences are operationally real, rather than feigned to give Pretoria the excuse of 'reaching a consensus', 'preparing the people for change' and similar classic poses in South Africa's negotiating position, is difficult to determine. Mr P.W. Botha's position within the National Party is not such that he can afford to be seen giving Namibia to 'the communists'. Yet three goals are emerging which South Africa's leadership seems to be pursuing with a degree of unanimity.

The principal goal appears to be to get out of Namibia at minimum cost before the military position or economy is critically undermined. The cost of the war after a major SWAPO offensive this year could rise to R750 million in 1982. A secondary objective is to preserve Namibia's economic links with the Republic and South Africa's political leverage after independence. Finally there is a need to avoid major psychological damage to white morale, defections to the Herstigte Nasionale Party (HNP) and the related boost to black resistance within South Africa. Thus while the principal goal could be achieved with free elections under the UN and a subsequent SWAPO government, the subsidiary goals could not, at least over the long term.

Different South African factions place different interpretations on ways to achieve each goal, and different weights on their importance. But none, rather predictably, sees how to achieve all at once, and none sees military defeat or economic collapse as imminent in Namibia. Procrastination therefore serves to unite the domestic National Party as well as buying time. In this sense internal disagreements in South Africa's National Party tend to lengthen the war.

Future negotiations over UN-supervised elections in Namibia are likely, therefore, to include a deceptive hidden agenda: the retention of Namibia as an economic dependency of South Africa, and the elimination of Angola as a threat to South Africa's 'security'. The first makes it improbable that SWAPO will leave the conference table with Walvis Bay as part of Namibia; the deep-water port is the subject of a separate Security Council resolution that implicitly leaves negotiations on its transfer until after independence. The second means that pressure will be put on the Angolan government over Cuban troops, and possibly the ANC, as part of the concessions required for South Africa's compliance with Resolution 435. Since Angola is ready to phase out Cuban troops once the UN Transition Assistance Group is in place, these demands may concentrate on the presence of the ANC. Any such linking of Namibian independence with South Africa's own internal political crisis is, of course, unjustified.

The USA and the 'total strategy'

It is the gravest misfortune for Namibia that the USA, which in 1919 successfully stopped South Africa simply annexing Namibia, now seems determined to impose conditions delivering the territory permanently into South Africa's economic orbit. The central themes of the Reagan administration's Africa policy — South Africa as a bulwark against communism, custodian of minerals required by America's military-industrial complex, the centre of a free enterprise system encompassing the southern region of the continent in a constellation of dependent states — are all, with different nuances, to be found in the policies of Pretoria's 'total strategy' theorists.

But these are not the themes of the EEC, which has contributed to the efforts of the front-line states and SADCC towards the struggle for economic liberation from the Republic, and which has held talks at several different levels with SWAPO. Nor are they those of the Contact Group as a whole, which has in the past striven to get Resolution 435 implemented, albeit at a high cost to SWAPO in concessions to South Africa and time, and lives, wasted. It remains to be seen whether the body of the Contact Group, led by the French foreign minister Cheysson, will be able to retain the United States in a united initiative or whether the price for unity will be a failure to resist Pretoria-inspired efforts to 'strengthen' the UN plan in Washington.

By mid-September 1981 such 'strengthened' plans were being negotiated again between Washington and Pretoria, and reports suggested some support from the front-line states and the Contact Group as a whole. The new proposals involved familiar concessions to South Africa: in particular, while SWAPO military units were required to remain in a foreign country, Angola, South African police and the 'South West Africa Defence Force' would remain in Namibia, apparently free to control the community during transition. Given the intimidatory role of the forces in the 1971 elections, a free and fair election under these conditions must be in serious doubt. The plan also left Walvis Bay in South Africa's hands and required constitutional guarantees to preserve the privileges of Namibia's whites. It was unclear whether these conditions — without even the promises of compensation and aid made to the Zimbabweans at Lancaster House — would be acceptable to SWAPO.

However there were indications that South Africa was again willing to accept a UN presence. The central theme of South Africa's position appeared to have shifted to the 'security' of Namibia's whites. Security and human rights denied to blacks for so long suddenly became the order of the day.

Ultimately the best guarantees for white settlers are a willingness to participate with a degree of self-sacrifice in the struggle for economic liberation that follows political independence. The security of Namibia's whites, as several German farmers saw in 1978 when they applied to join SWAPO believing independence near, lies in a strong government able to carry out its mandate to the Namibian people and not in search of scapegoats as expectations are unfulfilled. Today their welfare appears to be subordinate to the strategic goals of military planners in Washington and Pretoria. It might serve them better to begin working for one Namibia, one nation, than suffer the inexorable collapse of the DTA and spread of warfare throughout the territory that failure to reach a settlement may mean.

The most important requirement of any settlement, given the pattern of previous cycles of negotiations, is good faith on South Africa's side. This has still to be demonstrated in the present set of negotiations. These leave South Africa both the time and the room to manoeuvre and withdraw, as in the past, in order to try and consolidate DTA rule and monitor the impact of recent raids into southern Angola. It is clear that negotiations without the threat of rigorously applied sanctions have in the past been unable to bring about the required change in South Africa's position. Indeed South Africa's position hardened in early 1981 and she effectively created a buffer zone in southern Angola.

With the rapid intensification of the Namibian conflict inside Angola, the west must now urgently seek the implementation of Resolution 435 with more than half-hearted diplomatic pressure. Namibia and southern Angola, against all reason, have been turned by South Africa into a strategic battleground. Optimism is slipping away in Namibia, church sources indicate, as the people sense they have become the helpless victims of South African militarism. If the United States is seriously concerned at the Cuban presence in Angola, it must work to remove its cause, South Africa's military presence in Namibia and southern Angola. And, if its dangerous obsession with fighting the cold war in Africa is to be calmed, it might profitably heed the *Times* editorial of 31 August 1981: 'In the long run it is African nationalism itself that will defeat Soviet penetration'.

Appendix A

It is not the purpose of this appendix to give a comprehensive list of civilian killings by the SADF but to provide an example of the types of incidents in which civilians die. The British *Sunday Times* of 22 March 1981 gives details of one incident in which 11 villagers died after grenades were thrown into a kraal. A magistrate found that they had died as a result of SADF 'negligence'; no action was taken against troops. The *Windhoek Observer* of 4 April 1981 describes two massacres by a Ovambo 'home guard', one involving eight dead and 12 seriously wounded at Omashaka.

On 25 January 1981 a patrol of South African Defence Forces came upon a wedding reception at Onaalangate on the border between Uukwanyama and Ondonga near the Ondangua-Oshikango road. Present were two PLAN guerrillas. The patrol opened fire, killing one guerrilla, and the other ran off. The crowd dived for cover and lay prostrate on the ground whereupon the patrol opened fire on them again killing 15 and wounding about 12. The dead were as follows:

Eliye Kailiwa and her child
Alfeus Jakob
Andreas Moses
Mwatilifange Halweendo
Frida Moses (a pregnant woman)
Abraham Hangada
Frans Kakweno
Katombela
Hofni Vilho
Matheus Kamati
Fernando Shikokola
Kelista Hangula
The daughter of Shidjeni Nekongo (himself now missing).

Unlike the other three massacres reported since the beginning of 1981, this killing of innocent civilians has not been reported in any newspaper. It has been corroborated from two different sources inside Namibia.

The following account of the wounding of a young Namibian, also from sources inside Namibia, gives a further impression of the conduct of the war:

In February 1981 a 17 year-old called X was stopped at Onemedhiya by white soldiers of the SADF. He showed an identity card but his tax card showed no payment during the last year. He was taken to a tree under which was the corpse of a 12 year-old boy, R, stripped to his underpants and biting ants placed on his body. After forcing him to lie down next to the corpse, the troops moved off to stop a passing car and the boy crawled away. As he began running the troops noticed, opened fire and he was shot in the arm. He escaped and survived by binding up the wound to staunch the blood flow with palm leaves.

In February 1981, in another incident, Mr Y was stopped by a soldier and did not have an identity card with him. He was beaten and tortured with electric coils; to escape from the pain he gave the name of Mr Z as a collaborator with PLAN. Mr Z, a school teacher, was harassed by troops and police for the rest of the month. He had no contact with PLAN but the police threats resulted in his fleeing on 27 February.

(Information from sources inside Namibia)

Appendix B

Open letter from church leaders to the Secretary-General of the UN, January 1981.

1981 January 16th

His Excellency
Dr Kurt Waldheim
Secretary-General
New York, NY
United States of America

To Whom It May Concern

Your Excellency,

We, the leaders of the undermentioned Churches, having met in Windhoek on the 15th January, 1981 to re-assess the developments on the subjects of compulsory military service in our country, feel that it is now our imperative duty to inform the members of our church congregations as to the opinion that we as churches have unanimously agreed to.

We therefore remove the seal of confidentiality on our letter of Petition to the State President of the Republic of South Africa, despatched on the 29th October 1980, and make the said document public, basing our reasons therefore on the following grounds:

1 Apart from receiving a letter of acknowledgement of receipt, we have received no further communication from the addressee to date.

2 In spite of our petition, compulsory military service is being implemented and large numbers of young men have already been drafted ipso facto into the Territorial force for military training.

Confidential

Letter of Petition

His Excellency
The State President of the
Republic of South Africa
Pretoria

Re: **Compulsory Military Service in the Territory of SWA/Namibia**
The Following Documents Have Reference:

- Circular No.13 of 1980 dd. 30 September 1980 ex the Secretariat of the Department of National Education, Windhoek
- Proclamation AG 149 of 1980: Official Gazette extraordinary No.4300 dd. 17 October 1980
- Act 40/1857 as amended
- Act 44/1957 as amended

Your Excellency,

We, the leaders of the African Methodist Episcopal Church, the Anglican Church, the Evangelical Lutheran Church, the Evangelical Lutheran Owambokavango Church and the Roman Catholic Church, representing the majority of the population, met in Windhoek on the 22nd, 23rd, 24th and 25th of October 1980, to discuss the effects and repercussions of the abovementioned circular, Proclamation and Acts.

We are of the unanimous and informed opinion that if registration for compulsory call-up were to be proceeded with in the manner dictated by circular 13 of the Department of National Education, (which we feel is in any event ultra vires the power of the Department), then a very substantial number of parents and pupils will be alienated from the schools, of which some are run by the Churches, and a conflict situation will be created, not only between the Churches and their adherents, but also between governmental authority and the people generally.

It is our united opinion that we would find it extremely difficult to co-operate or support such directive and/or legislation without having certain clarifications made beforehand.

We therefore appeal to you as the signatory of Proclamation AG 149/80 to reconsider the effects that such legislation will have, not only on the lives of the people directly involved, but also on the security and stability of our nation.

1   In support of our appeal we humbly make the following submissions:

    1 (i) It is understandable, if not entirely desirable, that the Defence Act be made applicable to this Territory should there be the need to defend our country from the threat of an onslaught by a foreign power upon her sovereignty. However, in view of the

nature of the opposing factions involved in the present guerrilla war, the enlistment of SWA/Namibia nationals for compulsory military service would result in that war becoming a Civil War. The situation now being created is entirely different of the present position where armed incursion is combated by military personnel voluntarily enlisted from amongst the SWA/Namibian people.

1 (ii) The introduction of compulsory service at this stage of the settlement negotiations could be interpreted as being in direct conflict with and as a block to the much desired settlement through the medium of UN-supervised elections. We further beg leave to express our doubts on the compatability of the Proclamation AG 149 with the provision of the Mandate placed on the Territory of SWA/Namibia.

1 (iii) There is considerable confusion related to the matter of citizenship-qualification and rights in relationship to the sovereignty and independent Government of this Territory.

1 (iv) In view of the nature of the conflict situation and the agonies of conscience that will be forced on a large number of nationals, in particular in the Northern areas, it is doubtful whether the provisions of the Law are sufficiently adequate to deal with the matter of conscientious objection on a sympathetic basis.

1 (v) Likewise, the doubt is expressed as to the provision of adequate facilities in Law and in Defence Infrastructure for those who, on grounds of conscience, would opt for non-combatant military service.

1 (vi) It is respectfully submitted that the status quo, i.e. voluntary enlistment, would circumvent the problem listed in 1 (iii), (iv) and (v) above. However, should the response to voluntary enlistment not be adequate to supply the defence system, we beg to request that consideration be given to the possibility of this being a rejection by the majority of the people of the political 'status quo'.

2   We further wish to respectfully submit the possible consequences of the enforcement of compulsory military service.

2 (i) The immediate exodus of large numbers of our people, both men and women, coupled to the resultant dangers of injury and death as well as imprisonment from this 'illegal' activity.

2 (ii) The further polarisation of the people of this Territory at a time when consensus and reconciliation are being sought. This could well further escalate the proportions of a bloody, civil war and anarchy.

2 (iii) The increase of attacks on governmental institutions and installations, as well as military installations, and the requirement of large resources of time, equipment and man-power to protect these from such attacks.

2 (iv) The strong possibility of strikes emanating from educational

and industrial sectors must be borne in mind especially as the student boycott-tragedies are still very much a reality.

2 (v) Damage to the educational system, so vital to the future development of an emergent independent nation, would be enormous, as parents would withhold their children from schools in an attempt to protect them. To introduce compulsory education would prove futile as there would not be sufficient facilities or personnel to provide adequate schooling for all the population thus requiring it.

We therefore, in the light of the above, ask Your Excellency to review Proclamation AG 149 and seek alternate means to bring a cessation to the armed conflict by a peaceful and supervised electoral process in conjunction with the United Nations Organisation in terms of the provisions at their Proposals (Security Council Resolution 435, 1978 and subsequent agreements) and with an absolute minimum of delay.

We hold ourselves available to meet with you or your accredited representative at your convenience.

Your Excellency, we express our gratitude to you for considering our petition and assure you of our prayers for the guidance of Almighty God in the decisions that you, in co-operating with others, have to make on the future of our nation.

'Now may the Lord of Peace himself give you Peace at all times in all ways.' (*2 Thessalonians 3 v 16 (a)*).

With respect,

African Methodist Episcopal Church
Anglican Church
Evangelical Lutheran Church
Evangelical Lutheran Owambokavango Church
Roman Catholic Church

cc   *The Prime Minister of the Republic of South Africa*
      His Excellency the Administrator General of South West Africa/
      Namibia
PS   *Please direct correspondence to: The General Secretary, Council of*
      Churches in Namibia, PO Box 41, Tel: 061-37510, Windhoek 9000.

Appendix C

British Council of Churches statement on British mining in Namibia.

The following resolution was passed at the BCC Assembly meetings of October 1975 in regard to Namibia and the UK's mining interests in the territory:

The Assembly of the British Council of Churches

Welcomes the statement of British Government policy on Namibia made on 9 June 1975 and in particular the Government's desire 'to secure for the people of Namibia their full, free and independent status';

recalls the decrees of the UN Council for Namibia of 27 September 1974 designed to secure for the people of Namibia 'adequate protection of the natural wealth and resources of the territory which is rightfully theirs', and the action of the UN General Assembly of 13 December 1974 in requesting that the member States of the UN should ensure full compliance with that decree;

deplores the fact that the mineral resources of Namibia are being exploited by British firms and their subsidiaries; urges the British Government to undertake a thoroughgoing examination of the conditions under which mining operations are undertaken by British firms and their subsidiaries, and in particular of the wages and living conditions of their employees, and to publish their report.

Appendix D

'Counter Insurgency — A Way of Life', SWA/Namibia
Information Service, Windhoek 1980.

COUNTER INSURGENCY
- A WAY OF LIFE -

tle and undermining because of the use of propaganda. The youth is the target and their particular field of interest is employed. Pop music, films and literature is subtly applied to mask the true identity and aims of the aggressor. Moral codes are gradually and unobtrusively decayed and drugs are presented as perfectly harmless. By these means a healthy spirit, soul and body is affected and the victim falls prey to the insurgent. Southern Africa is now the terrain where the insurgent operates with the aim of affecting every facet of daily life, to cause disruption and chaos and to confuse the local population to the extent that the military wing of the terrorist movement can attempt to take over control of the country.

This total assault requires total resistance (by each and everyone) on a basis organised by those in authority in the particular country. It requires a continuous and controlled reciprocal relationship between the economic, political, military, diplomatic, and cultural facets of the state. These means of countering insurgency is at its most effective when it is executed in the form of a total strategy.

In the first place total strategy must be a preventive measure because preventing an insurgent attack saves lives and money. However, in certain respects a solid front of opposition must be presented to the enemy and this requires from everybody, also from the ordinary citizen, a larger measure of involvement and contribution than merely following the progress of the war in a newspaper.

International involvement in insurgency (like the apparent support SWAPO enjoys at the United Nations) is a relatively new development in the conflict.

This makes new demands on the community, and peace, stability and harmony within the country is the decisive factor in regard to whether or not a country survives the onslaught.

The purpose of this publication is to offer the reader a better insight into the nature of the onslaught against the country. It is also aimed at enlightening those who erroneously feel uninvolved in the conflict and to indicate what they can do to contribute to a total resistance to the onslaught.

Foreword

Insurgency is the military term for the infiltration of terrorists from neighbouring countries to the country which is their target. The insurgents (terrorists) have one primary aim and that is to disrupt the existing Government and the law and order of the country by means of violence, as well as an assault on the spiritual values of the local population. By these means they aim to gain control of the country, its peoples and its riches.

A "total insurgency onslaught" is the term used for this threat which is aimed against everything and everybody regardless of race or colour. The big danger is that the onslaught is not always visible, but is sub-

The main method of attack is intangible. The insurgent concentrates on the sensational in order to spread his message.

The image of SWAPO in South African propaganda.

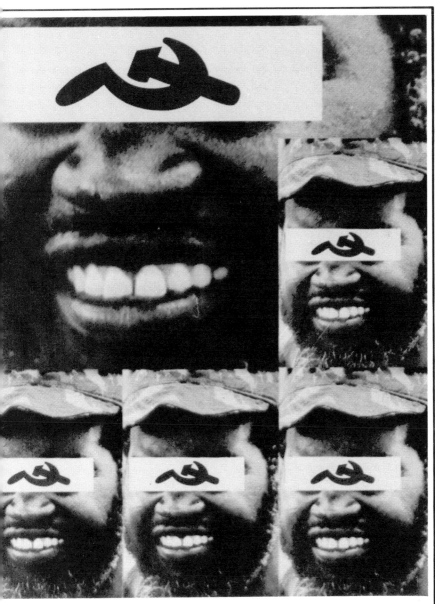

The insurgent aims to overthrow the present form of Government in order to establish a regime of his own choice. To him it does not matter how many lives are lost in the process.

deprived of yet another exploitable situation.

The process of education starts within the family circle and is continued at educational institutions. The forming of a sound character, the acquiring of knowledge and a process of awareness regarding the nature, aims and dangers of communist insurgency, and an unshakeable Christian faith can best assist the process of counter-insurgency. A resistance to the dangers of indoctrination by the insurgent can, by these means, become an inherent part of the national character.

The most important aim of counter-insurgency is a happy community and the foundation for this lies in the family circle, educational institutions and the church.

Men and women of all cultures receive their training here to enable them to contribute to counter-insurgency in all sectors of the community.

National Security, a pagan religion in Christian dress: 'an unshakeable Christian Faith can assist the process of counter-insurgency . . . The strong practised Christian religion is . . . the key to a contented, regulated community'.

The role of the faith in God in regard to the onslaught

The strong, practised Christian religion is pre-eminently the key to a contented, regulated community which strives for a peaceful existence, also for the generations to follow. In the counter-insurgency struggle, the insurgent can succeed in having a short-term, negative influence on the population in regard to material aspects. He can damage the economy and achieve limited and temporary success in the military field. But there is one single factor and the most important of all — belief in Jesus Christ and in God — which can never be affected by the enemy.

The inner strength which we receive in the form of faith in the supreme being of Almighty God, plays a far-reaching role. For the soldier on the battlefield it is a shield and a weapon, and for the family at home it is a source of strength and trust.

We cannot stand up to the enemy onslaught without the steadfastness of our belief. Everyone who believes in the Lord God can reject the moral onslaught and false promises of the insurgent. By means of the daily use of the armament of God, the morale of a nation is strengthened.

Prayer is one of our mightiest weapons and strengthens the individual and the nation. Prayer for the preservation of our Christian way of life; for a neighbour in need; for the soldier in the tremendous task he has to perform; creates an invincible inner strength.

The insurgent has no weapon against the faith in God

By means of propaganda he attempts to proclaim that religion is used as a means of enslaving the nation and making them subservient. They claim that religion is just another means employed by the "suppressor" who is supported by the "discriminating dispensation" to suppress the underprivileged. Yet, only the unenlightened and those who have not yet discovered the truth of the belief in God, will fall prey to these arguments put forward by the insurgent. That is why the spreading of the word of God should be a continuous process.

Conclusion

Taking all aspects into consideration, the collective, decisive factor in countering the insurgency threat is the invincible will to win, both spiritually and in regard to the maintaining of the present dispensation of law and order. The main onslaught of the insurgent is intangible and is directed at corroding the cultural values, courage, daring and determination of the population. Various factors can contribute to providing a favourable climate for murder and

Retention of the Christian belief forms an invincible bastion against insurgency.

Appendix E

Statement by the Namibian Council of Churches to the US Delegation on its Visit to Namibia 12 June 1981.

The Council of Churches in Namibia (CCN), representing more than 75% of Christians in this country, is continuously committed to work for justice, peace and reconciliation.

It is out of this commitment and firm desire to see peace that the Council of Churches in Namibia has been especially concerned over the years about a peaceful and just solution of the political problems of our country and through various actions has supported the implementation of the United Nations Security Council Resolution 435 (1978).

We had appealed on numerous occasions to the United Nations, South Africa and the five western countries (USA, West Germany, Britain, France and Canada) for an immediate implementation of the UN plan. It is our conviction that this would prevent the escalation of violence and bloodshed and the growing hatred amongst the people of Namibia.

While there are now talks about the protection of the rights (privileges) of minorities, we are dumbfounded to learn that the long overdue right of the majority of the nation to determine their own future and to become independent seems to be a secondary matter for some western governments. Thus, the Council of Churches in Namibia believes in the same rights for all Namibians as declared in the UN Declaration of Human Rights.

It is in the interests of all our people, therefore, that every effort be made to immediately resume discussions aiming for a cease-fire date, and a start of implementation in accordance with Security Council Resolution 435 (1978). We reiterate that it is our continued conviction and confidence that the only practical peaceful solution lies in the hands of the United Nations.

We feel that any party involved in the negotiations who does not have the faith to co-operate in the national interest and who is insensitive to the suffering of our people should be held responsible for any failure of a peaceful solution.

We therefore again appeal to our congregation and all Christians throughout the world to pray without ceasing for the peace of Namibia (Col:4:2).

Appendix F

Statement by the Evangelical Lutheran Ovambokavango Church and Evangelical Lutheran Church in South West Africa (Rheinish Mission) on the 10th Anniversary of the Open Letter to the Prime Minister of South Africa Mr B.J. Vorster on 30 June 1971.

On 30 June, 1971, 10 years ago, the Evangelical Lutheran Ovambokavango Church and the Evangelical Lutheran Church in South-West-Africa (Rheinish Mission) wrote an open letter to the then Prime Minister of South Africa, Mr B.J. Vorster. In this letter these Churches expressed the urgent wish that 'in terms of the declarations of the World Court and in co-operation with the UNO of which South Africa is a member, your Government will seek a peaceful solution to the problems of our land and will see to it that Human Rights be put into operation and that South-West Africa may become a self-sufficient and independent State'.

Despite numerous decisions and resolutions by the United Nations and South Africa and despite the cry that the people of Namibia should determine their own future, ten long years has past without giving them the opportunity to make this decision themselves.

Already in January 1976 the UN Security Council, through its resolution 385, called for free and fair elections in Namibia under UN supervision and control.

Since then the situation in Namibia and for the Namibian people has turned from bad to worse. The Namibian people have become the play-ball in the process and many hundreds of them, yes thousands, are being killed in a situation that has become a war situation.

We strongly confirm the position taken by the Executive Committee of the Council of Churches in Namibia as stated on 15 January, 1981: 'We feel strongly that minor matters concerning status and/or partiality/impartiality should not be allowed to effect the peaceful future of our nation and that every effort should be made to rise above such pettiness. Endless negotiations on such minor grounds prolong the acute agony and suffering of our people, as they only increase the numbers of our people who died as a result of the war'.

81

We once again appeal to the South African Government in co-operation with the UN, as ten years ago, to give the Namibian people the opportunity to determine their own future through a free and fair election.

It should not be allowed that the fear for the results of such an election, which would establish the will of the people, should deprive a nation from the right to determine their future.

We will call upon the members of our Churches and all Christians to continually pray for a just society and the genuine independence of our country.

Signed:

Bishop Dr K. Dumeni Evangelical Lutheran Ovambokavango Church
Preses H. Frederik Evangelical Lutheran Church in SWA (RS)

Windhoek 30/06/1981

Suggested Further Reading

H. Hunke & J. Ellis

Torture — a cancer in our society BCC-CIIR, London 1978.

J. Ellis

Elections in Namibia? BCC-CIIR, London 1979.

R.H. Green

From Südwestafrika to Namibia: the Political Economy of Transition Scandinavian Institute of African Studies Research Report No 58, Uppsala 1981.

R.H. Green, K. Kiljunen & M.L. Kiljunen

Namibia: The Last Colony Longman, London 1981.

International Defence and Aid Fund

Namibia — The Facts London 1980.

World Council of Churches

Documentation on UN Pre-implementation Meeting on Namibia Geneva, January 1981.

SOME OTHER TITLES AVAILABLE FROM CIIR

South Africa in the 1980s: CIIR 1980 41pp **75p**

South Africa: A Test Case for the West by Peter Walshe CIIR 1980 20pp **50p**

Elections in Namibia? CIIR and BCC 1979 63pp **50p**

From Rhodesia to Zimbabwe Series ed. Roger Riddell CIIR 9 vols, 1977-1980.

Foreign Companies and International Investment in Zimbabwe by Duncan Clarke CIIR and Mambo Press 1980 275pp **£4**

Political Change in South Africa: Britain's Responsibility: BCC 1979 **80p***

Arms For Apartheid: British Military Collaboration with South Africa by Pat Fitzsimons and Jonathan Bloch Christian Concern for Southern Africa 1981 **£2***

A Code for Misconduct by Barbara Rogers Christian Concern for Southern Africa 1980 **£2***

British Banks and South Africa by Rodney Stares based on research by Martin Bailey Christian Concern for Southern Africa 1979 **£1.80***

Britain's Economic Links with South Africa: Christian Concern for Southern Africa 1979 **£1.50***

Mambo Press Socio-Economic Series — details available from CIIR.

Prices do not include postage and packing. A full list of CIIR publications is available, free of charge, on request.

Also available from BCC, 2 Eaton Gate, London SW1.